Model Vegan on Weight loss: How I went from a size 18 to 8 in 3 months

DUSHENKA SILBERFARB

ISBN-10: 1494817616
ISBN-13: 978-1494817619

DEDICATION

This book is dedicated to my family, especially my mother, and my friends. Without you, this book would not exist.

CONTENTS

Acknowledgments   i

1   Introduction   1

2   My Story   11

3   Best Breakfasts   17

4   Salads, Sides and other Accompaniments   21

5   Best Breads   75

6   One Dish Wonders   84

7   Curries, Soups and Stews   106

8   Delightful Dinners   137

9   Desserts You Won't Have to Desert   160

ACKNOWLEDGMENTS

It is impossible to thank all the people that contribute to the making of a book. Nevertheless there are key people who contributed enormously to the finished product. My mother has taught me everything I know about health and being healthy. My sister Aja, tested countless recipes and created youtube videos of the recipes. My sister Jeselle tested countless recipes again, and created a website for my books, www.modelvegan.com. Many, many friends purchased self-published versions of this book and gave me feedback on everything from recipes instructions to the title! Lastly my husband Andrew and daughter Elena have served as cooking inspirations and fabulous dishwashers and kitchen helpers. Thank you!

1 INTRODUCTION

My mother is a health nut. She's been studying nutrition, physiology and medicine since long before I was born. Unlike many of our relatives, she is not even a little bit overweight and when we go places together, people frequently mistake her for my sister. She has a lot of rules about eating. Twice, I have decided to eat "whatever I want, whenever I want," and each time I got really fat. Each time I reverted to my mother's diet, the weight came off easily and effortlessly without feelings of deprivation. The first time I returned to the diet on which I was raised, I didn't notice any change in my physical size in the first 90 days. I noticed I needed less sleep and had more energy. People around me noticed I was happier and nicer to be around. The week after 90 days, I went from a size 18 to a size 16. The next week I went from a size 16 to a size 14. People I saw on a weekly basis commented, "Your melting!" and so I was. I continued to lose about a size a week until I hit my naturally healthy weight of a size 8. The second time I left the diet, gained a bunch of weight and then returned, I wasn't tracking clothing size, but rather I was tracking pounds. Again, the first three months, I stayed the same weight. However, after those three months, I lost five pounds a week until I'd lost a total of 65 pounds and my BMI went from the obese range to the middle of the normal range.

I use the word diet to describe the collection of rules my mother taught us to follow or suffer the consequences, not in the sense of something you do for a short period of time to lose a lot of weight. While three months seems to be the time I need to see physical results, Dr. Neal Barnard, who incidentally advocates the same diet on which my mother raised me, invites people to try the diet for 21 days and has found, in many cases, that after just three weeks, people see such dramatic results, they are unwilling to return to their previous way of eating. Now Dr. Barnard works with people who eat the standard American diet which includes meat, dairy, sugar, caffeine, alcohol. None of those were ever a part of my diet, but there are many recipes in The Model Vegan that I have invented for birthdays and other celebrations that do not support weight-loss, and that I know from personal experience add to your waistline if you let them become a regular part of your diet. My aunt Bonnie, has the additional health challenge of having Downs Syndrome. Obesity is frequently paired with Downs Syndrome and Bonnie was no exception. When Bonnie first came to live with us, she was as wide as her five feet height. We never limited her portions. We never forced her to exercise and for two years after coming to live with us and following our diet, she maintained her spherical proportions. And then, after two years, she began losing weight quite rapidly until her body was a child's size 10. Suddenly, instead of having to buy special clothes for her and have them tailored, if I saw something cute in a child's size ten, I could buy it for her and know that it would fit her even before she tried it on! She has remained that size with the exception of the year Andrew and I married. That year, while Andrew and I went on our honeymoon and moved across the country, Bonnie stayed with a relative who doesn't eat the way my mother does and in those three weeks, she gained three pants sizes. When she came home and resumed our diet, she returned to a child's size ten, but it took five months for her to finish losing the weight she gained in those three weeks. I don't know if you will see changes in three weeks, three months, five months, or two years! But I know this diet works, and works consistently, to produces health, vitality and weight-loss. As an aside, it will also help someone who has trouble gaining weight, gain weight to their proper size because it helps the body take full advantage of the available nutrition, but I'm assuming you are not concerned ab out gaining and maintaining your weight since you are reading the Model Vegan on Weight-loss.

I have noticed that how you do anything is how you do everything. When I stop paying attention to healthy habits and eat foods that are not on my diet and gain weight, my car is also full of trash and the windows are dirty. Clutter is in every room of my house and there is usually one or more relationship in my life that is causing me suffering and pain. The beautiful thing is that doing something in any of these areas, thoroughly cleaning one shelf in one closet or washing and vacuuming my car, forgiving someone that I am harboring anger and resentment towards, or going on a juice fast for a day will trigger action in all the other areas and in short order, my body looks and feels good, I have a clean, peaceful environment, and I feel loved by the people I care about and confident that they know and feel loved by me. In this book we are not going to talk about cleaning, or give advice on presencing love. We are going to talk about food, because you picked up the cookbook to read. Allors.

Growing up there were several rules of eating that my mother enforced vigorously. The two I remember having the most difficulty with were "No drinking while eating," and "No proteins at the same time as carbohydrates." My Dad would have a glass of water with dinner and would sometimes melt cheese on corn tortillas. "But those are against the RULES!!!!" my three year old self complained. "I want to break the rules, too!" I thought rebelliously. As an older, wiser version of myself, I realize that water dilutes the digestive fluids and makes it harder for the stomach to do its job. My mother would call us to the kitchen about 20 minutes before each meal to have a glass of water so that we wouldn't be thirsty during the meal and I know that when we sat down for dinner we weren't really thirsty – we just wanted to be like Dad.

I also have learned that alkaline digestive fluids are needed to digest carbohydrates and acidic digestive fluids are needed to digest proteins so chemically, the acidic and basic fluids released by the presence of carbs and proteins cause neither to be digested well (since acid and base will combine to form a neutral substance.) As a little kid, I just knew it "didn't mix," and to eat them together was to break the rules.

Rules that were easy to follow were: if eating melon, only eat one kind of melon at a time. Mom would let us eat an entire watermelon if we wanted to, but once we had that first bite of melon, the only thing that we would eat for at least an hour after the last bite was melon – the same kind of melon we had taken that first bite of. Later I read there were studies done on people who thought they were allergic to melons but it turns out that when they only ate one kind of melon, their "allergic reaction" went away.

As a little kid, my mother explained that when you combine your foods improperly, they cannot be digested properly and gas results. I now know that when foods which enter the stomach require different digestive fluids, one fluid will be "stronger" than the other but neither will be very effective and if you do eat something like beans with fruit, the fluids required to digest the beans, causes the fruit to rot. Rotten food breaks down into methane and sulfur gases which either stay in the stomach and causes pain in the form of cramping or passes through the intestines and is released as flatulence. Methane smells like dung and sulfur smells like rotten eggs. Neither smell is pleasant! As a kid, the thought of releasing flatulence which would let one of my siblings know that I had broken the rules was a large enough deterrent that I had no desire to mix any sort of sweet (whether it be a piece of fruit or a piece of dessert) with proteins or carbohydrates.

Another rule that was easy to follow, largely because as a kid I was never placed in a tempting situation, was: do not combine sugar with fat. When you do so, the fat molecules bond with the sugar molecules and your body can't break them down so your body stores them near the epidermis, and we know these structures as fat. Now, think about it. Every diet you ever read says, "Don't eat dessert," or "limit your intake of dessert." When you make cookies, what is the first thing you do? Cream the sugar with the fat. When baking a cake – what goes into it? Sugar and fat. Ice cream is made from? Sugar and fat. If your body cannot digest sugars when combined with fats, does it make sense that dessert isn't food and you can eat an entire box of cookies and still feel hungry? Try eating an entire 5 pound bag of carrots. By carrot number 5, I've usually had enough.

One of the things my mother did that I think was really smart was that dinners consisted of either a carbohydrate or protein dish, generous helpings of one vegetable and a salad at the end to polish it off. She said that sometimes the mind gets confused between hunger and the desire to try a new taste. If there are only 3 things to taste it's easier to tell when you are still hungry and when you just want to taste the next dish. For example mom would serve beans, rice and salad. Or she would make potatoes with peas and a salad, or spaghetti with marinara sauce and sliced cucumbers or carrots, vegetable soup with cornbread or biscuits and a salad. At lunch time, the salad might be the lunch, especially if it had a protein like avocado or sunflower seeds.

Another thing she instilled in us was to only eat until we were no longer hungry. Oprah's fitness coach, Bob Greene, has a hunger scale that goes from being weak and light-headed from hunger to being so full you feel nauseous. He recommends putting your fork down when you reach either "comfortable. You're more or less satisfied, but could eat a little more" or when you reach "perfectly comfortable. You feel satisfied." I don't ever recall feeling weak and light-headed from hunger. I don't even recall feeling uncomfortably full, much less nauseous! I blame my mother's training, "Only eat until you are no longer hungry...Are you still hungry or do you just want more? If you are still hungry, go ahead and have some more (of whatever we were just eating). If you are no longer hungry, you can eat more, later, when you are hungry again." Occasionally I would say, "I don't want more (whatever we were just eating)! I want (something else) instead!" My mother would infallibly reply "If you don't want (whatever we were just eating), then you are not really hungry. You are probably bored. Why don't you go play/read/work on puzzles/do something away from the table and the kitchen while your food is digesting? In three hours, after you have digested what you've just eaten, you can have something else." Three hours is a long time for little kids to wait, but that is how long it takes to digest proteins or carbohydrates. Melons or fruits can take an hour if they are eaten by themselves, which of course, is the best way to eat them!

Another rule that I never really noticed as being important until I stopped observing it was that we could only eat sitting down at the table. We never had the debate about eating dinner in front of the TV, because the TV was always in the living room and food was always served in the dining room. We did not eat in the kitchen or the bedroom or the hallway or on our way out the door. We never had to run through the rooms collecting dishes when it was time to do dishes because if we were eating, whether it was dinner or an afternoon snack, we were seated together at the dining room table and we all said grace beforehand. As we got older mother added the rule, "Do not make food only for yourself! If you are hungry, chances are, other people are hungry too. If you are making food, you must make enough for everyone." And this rule reinforced the established pattern of only eating while seated at the dining room table and of praying first. Human being have a need for ritual, whether it is saying grace or taking a moment of silence before the meal. Taking this time before every meal sends signals to the body "It's time to eat now!" and contributes to your enjoyment as does chewing slowly and taking the time to savor each bite. When you wolf down your food or eat standing up, you don't really taste it. You also don't give your stomach a chance to signal your brain, "I'm full now." This process can take up to twenty minutes. So say grace before eating so that love and blessing can flow into the food. Savor each bite, loving the way the flavors and textures feel in your mouth and after twenty minutes, if you feel like seconds you can ask yourself, "Are you really hungry or do you just want more?" You'll know the answer. And if you are really hungry, go ahead and have seconds. If you just want more, know that you have it again later when you are hungry again. It will still be there for you!

When my friends ask me about diet or weight loss the first thing I tell them is to replace all carbohydrates with whole grain versions of what they were eating before. Mother never ever ever let us eat anything made from white flour or unbleached flour because she explained that the whole grain contained vitamins and minerals needed to digest it and when you ate white flour, it would pull the vitamins from where ever in the body they happened to be and most of them were found in bones. She also made us glue from white flour and water to make paper mache and explained that in the same way the white flour forms a glue to stick the papers together, when you eat it, it forms a glue in your intestines, coating them and preventing other food from being digested properly. The image of intestines coated with glue always deters me from accepting when someone who doesn't know how I eat offers me something made from white flour.

My mother also never let us drink carbonated beverages because even if they didn't have sugar, and they almost all do, the carbonic acid that made them fizzy contributes to osteoporosis later in life. In the book Alkalize or Die, by Theodore Baroody, he writes that soda causes the body to build up acidic waste, no matter who made the soda. As an experiment try cutting out all carbonated beverages for 90 days (one day at a time). When my husband did this, he lost 3 inches from around his waist in two months — just from ending his soda consumption!

The next thing I advise my friends who ask is to remove all di-saccharides from your diet. Common di-saccharides are sucrose, high fructose corn syrup, organic cane sugar, organic beet sugar, maltose, lactose. Fructose is a mono-saccharide and the body processes it the same way it processes carbohydrates. High fructose corn syrup, however, has less than 14% fructose. The rest of the components are dextrose and it has a rating of 89 on the glycemic index as opposed to fructose whose rating is only 32. The only thing worse than di-saccharides are artificial sweeteners such as saccharine, aspartame, splenda, equal, sweet and low. The body can process complex carbohydrates, polysaccharides, and simple sugars, mono-saccharides. In fact, when the body digests polysaccharides, it does so by breaking them down into mono-saccharides. Unfortunately, most of the sugar sold today is beet sugar or cane sugar, both of which are di-saccharides. Di-saccharides not only spike the blood sugar with all the detriment that entails, but also stress the liver and pancreas. The body spends a great deal of time and energy trying to break the di-saccharide down into a mono-saccharide and eventually gives up (because the bond is too strong to break) and stores the disaccharide in fat cells. Some disaccharides are actually worse than others. High fructose corn syrup, for example, produces a similar chemical reaction in the brain to the ingestion of cocaine. No wonder we are never satisfied with "just a taste." I am glad there is so much information available about HFC that the industry has lobbied to change the name. Fortunately, their petition was denied which is important for people how are trying to make positive choices about their health.

Unfortunately, the information about HFC has tainted the reputation of fructose, a simple sugar found in fruit that is quite easily digested and useful to your body in small quantities. While we are on the subject of sugar, I went to a "regular" grocery store while on vacation recently because the local health food store was closed and I was told the local grocery store had quite a selection of organic and healthy foods. I looked up and down every aisle, including the so called healthy aisles and the only product I was willing to buy in the entire store was white vinegar which I use for laundry and cleaning, only. If those products are what people refer to when they say to avoid fruit juice and carbohydrates, then by all means, avoid them! I wouldn't touch them with a ten foot pole! But please, don't lose the distinction between mono-saccharides which are useful and beneficial and di-saccharides and also between polysaccharides (whole grains and starchy vegetables) and poor imitations (white rice and bread) that take away nutrients from the body and cause you to gain weight.

The next thing I advise friends is to take the USANA HealthyPak every day without fail and drink lots of water. Unfortunately, we live in an environment saturated with toxins. When the body encounters a toxin, it wraps it in fat molecules and stores it on your hip, or butt, or wherever you tend to accumulate weight. It's no longer sufficient to just eat really healthfully. The nutrients that were found in fresh fruits and vegetables 50-100 years ago are simply not available in the same quantities of fruits and vegetables today. Taking the HealthyPak and drinking water gives your body the nutritional support to flush the toxins and heal itself. If you don't drink water or get the proper nutritional support, the chances of losing weight quickly are greatly diminished.

Sometimes eating exclusively whole grains, removing soda, artificial sweeteners combined with water and the HealthyPak is sufficient. But let's say you want to follow the diet that I used to go from an 18 to an 8 in three months, and stay there. In that case you will want to eat exclusively whole grains, remove soda, artificial sweeteners, drink your water, take your HealthyPak vitamins twice daily, **and** observe the following basic diet rules.

1. Eat acids and starches at separate meals. Acids neutralize the alkaline medium required for starch digestion and the result is fermentation and indigestion.

2. Eat protein foods and carbohydrate foods at separate meals. Protein foods require an acid medium for digestion.

3. Eat but one kind of protein food at a meal.

4. Eat proteins and acid foods at separate meals. The acids of acid foods inhibit the secretion of the digestive acids required for protein digestion. Undigested protein putrefies in bacterial decomposition and produces some potent poisons.

5. Eat sugars (fruits) and proteins at separate meals.

6. Eat sugars (fruits) and starchy foods at separate meals. Fruits undergo no digestion in the stomach and are held up if eaten with foods that require digestion in the stomach.
7. Eat melons alone. They combine with almost no other food.

8. Desert the desserts. Eaten on top of meals, they lie heavy on the stomach, requiring no digestion there, and ferment. Bacteria turn them into alcohols and vinegars and acetic acids.

So in terms of diet, what does that look like? Well, on the Healthyblast diet,

I take the USANA HealthPak product every day, twice a day with breakfast and with dinner. I also drink ask many ounces of filtered water as half my current weight. For example, if I weighed 200 pounds, I would drink 100 ounces of filtered water a day. I have breakfast several hours after waking. Three to four hours after breakfast, I will have lunch and then about five hours later I will eat dinner. I find that taking the USANA HealthyPak daily and cooking at home instead of going out, I get the nutrients my body needs and I have an internal motivation to stick to the eating habits that my mother raised us with. If I do feel hungry for a snack I will eat carrots or sugar snap peas or a piece of bread with peanut butter. Where do you find the USANA HealthPak? www.dushenka.usana.com

I find that having staples on hand is very useful. The staples I always have in my kitchen are several different whole grain flours, corn meal, fructose, non-aluminum baking powder, oats, dried basil, red chili powder, ginger, turmeric, brown mustard seeds, sesame seeds, black sesame seeds, coriander, cinnamon, ground cloves, whole nutmeg, cumin, sea salt, sunflower or safflower oil, cold pressed virgin olive oil, onions, firm organic non-gmo tofu, lemons, and whatever fruits and vegetables look the most tasty and fresh. The latter chapters of this book has recipes for foods that I eat that are combined properly and taste really good!

A note about flours:
Unless specifically noted, the type of flour used in this book isn't critical to the recipe turning out. Whole wheat pastry flour tastes and looks different from Kamut flour or whole grain spelt flour, but the recipes do not need to be modified to accommodate the different flours. None of the recipes in this book will work well with white flour or "all-purpose flour" or "unbleached flour. All of them have been created specifically with whole grain flours in mind and using a non-whole grain flour will lead to a pasty sticky mess. Before discovering that I am quite allergic to wheat, my go to flour was organic whole wheat pastry flour, preferably Bob's Red Mill which is stone ground from a soft white wheat, as opposed to the red wheat many wheat flours are made from. Stone ground flours preserve the oils in the flours, while milling with metal blades tends to denature the oils due to the heat of friction from cutting, as opposed to grinding. Once it was clear that I could not eat wheat without experiencing significant physical pain, I have used primarily spelt flour or kamut flour in my baking. Spelt flour has sharply shaped grains that tend to cut through gluten so it produces a more crumbly product. To me, it also has a more earthy, nutty flavor than wheat or kamut flour. Kamut flour is higher in protein and fat than modern wheat flours and produces a softer baked good than spelt or whole wheat. Since spelt and kamut are both types of wheat, they contain gluten and are not

suitable for gluten free diets. I am still experimenting with gluten free flour mixtures. I have found rice flour to be grainy on its own. Buckwheat and soy flours both have strong after tastes. The after taste of the soy flour is masked if it is less than half the total amount of flour used and I have found a fourth to be an even better quantity. Even a small amount of buckwheat, however, imparts the buckwheat flavor to whatever you are making so Ployes are the only recipe that I enjoy using buckwheat flour in.

A few notes about technique:
I wouldn't have thought to include this until I read it somewhere as a non-obvious step.-All the sifting in these recipes is to aerate the flours and thoroughly mix the dry ingredients. After sifting whole grain flours, there may be a few grits left in the sifter. Do NOT throw these away! Simply turn the sifter upside down and tap it to get all the good stuff into the batter and then proceed with the recipe.

When the recipe says to "roll out" the dough, pull a golf ball or ping pong ball sized piece of dough off the main ball of dough. Toss the ball in flour so it isn't sticky. Shape it into a smooth ball. Place it on your work surface and flatten with the palm of your hand or with a back and forth motion of the rolling pin. When the dough is flat, flip it over and rotate it 90 degrees. Roll the pin forward and back over the flipped dough and repeat until a round flat shape about 1/8-1/4 inch thick is formed.

Never soak beans before cooking them. Soaking them leaches out all the yummy nutrients. When using dry beans, wash them and put them straight into the pot for cooking.

Carefully remove all the dirt from root vegetables but never peel them. Some of the best nutrients are found in or next to the skins.

The recipe no more makes the chef than the prayer makes the saint! Variations in food caused by different growing conditions or even the weather on the day you are cooking will cause variations in your results. As long as you trust your eyes, nose and mouth, this is a very good thing.

My Cooking Ethics
I ask myself, "Would I personally be willing to do what was done to get the ingredients to the table?" If I am not, I don't eat it. This excludes all meat, poultry, fish, eggs, dairy, synthetic dyes, artificial flavors, transfatty acids, white flour, bleached or bromated foods.

When I'm feeling lazy I will eat:

fruit (apples, nectarines, peaches, grapes, bananas, cherries)
juice (carrot or orange)
melon (watermelon or cantelope)
frozen juice (apple juice, grape juice, pineapple-coconut juice)
frozen fruit (bananas, grapes, plums, blueberries, cherries, black berries, strawberries)
smoothies (apple juice + banana + frozen berries)
fresh berries (blueberries, strawberries, raspberries)
hummus and Veggies (cooked garbanzo beans in the food processor with garlic, lemon, olive oil, salt eaten as a dip with romaine lettuce, carrots, jicama or peas - anything that can grab the hummus)
veggies (jicama, carrots, lettuce)
nuts (Brazil nuts, roasted cashew, raw almond, roasted pistachio)
sorbet: frozen strawberries or raspberries in the food processor with enough apple juice (about 2 tablespoons) to make them a sorbet rather than chopped frozen fruit.
sandwiches
cereal
Remember, the secret ingredient to all of these recipes is love! Love the food as you buy it. Love it as you prepare it and love it as you eat it! Choose the freshest ingredients and prepare them immediately. If you find yourself stopping by the market on the way home from work, remember that 5 minutes at the grocery store will save you hours in the kitchen when you get home. After food has begun to loose its freshness, the best sauces and preparation in the world won't make it taste good, but if the food starts out fresh and tasty, with little or no preparation, a fresh and tasty meal can be made.

DIET FOR TRAVELERS
When you are traveling, you can still follow our diet. Take your HealthyPak with you when you go.

When you are ordering lunch or dinner remember the most important rule is to never eat things that are sweet with things that aren't sweet. For example, eat toast with butter, but not jam. Snack on an apple or on crackers, but never on apples and crackers. And of course, desert the dessert.

The second most important rule to remember is not to mix complete proteins with carbohydrates. Eat tofu with salad, but not rice. Eat pasta with vegetables and, of course, completely eschew all meat and cheese.

Do the best you can and remember to love yourself and drink lots of water!

2 MY STORY

In working with what is, rather than what I wanted to be, the very challenges that in the moment caused me to feel like my life was over, have inspired me to give myself a complete make-over and explore new cuisines and new ways of being that bring a great deal of joy, vitality and health into my life. I read once that it is easier to get divorced, find a new husband and remain happily married to that new husband than it is to change the fundamental eating habits that govern our life. This book is written for anyone with a food challenge or who wants to lose weight or who would like to make a radical dietary change for any reason. May my story of how I turned the biggest ow! of my life into a wow! help you to do the same.

The following are excerpts of my personal journey and included to encourage people with food allergies or who just want to make a shift to make the changes for living this new reality.

Remembering that time, the advice I would have liked to have received and that would have made the biggest difference for me is if someone had sat me down, looked me in the eye and said, *"This is not the end of the world; your life is not over; it is not the case that you will never eat another dessert or your favorite comfort foods ever again."* Your tastes will change and what was once so gripping you could not imagine life without it as being worthwhile will, at some point be completely unappealing and there will be new and wonderful foods that taste amazing and make you feel like a superhero!

11

1-30-2008

We've now been wheat and dairy free for about 6 weeks now. My loving husband went on the wheat-free, dairy-free diet with me because he loves me and wants to support me in achieving optimal health. The first 2 weeks were the hardest. I cried. a lot. I think it's because my body was addicted to wheat and dairy in the same way that a body gets addicted to other substances that are bad for it. Also difficult was the mental shift from buying 5lbs of organic whole wheat pastry flour for $3.99, to buying 1/4 lb of kamut, spelt or barley flour for anywhere from $6 to $12. I was feeling like that was a SIGNIFICANT increase in grocery spending and somewhat resistant to making that change. Andrew argued that he's highly invested in my body and would rather spend $100 a pound on flour than return to the health crisis precipitated by eating wheat and dairy and that I'm worth every penny and more. Since Andrew and I have been on the wheat-free, dairy-free diet and made sure to rotate our foods so that we don't eat the same food with-in 3 days, (ie if we have rice, rice pasta, rice crackers, we won't eat anything with rice again for 3 days) the first thing Andrew noticed was the my skin cleared up. It wasn't just that I no longer had any blemishes, according to Andrew, my entire skin everywhere feels softer and creamier and he just wants to touch it all the time. The first thing I noticed is that my body is starting to look like it did when I was dancing 8 hours a day and I haven't even started a regular exercise routine yet. The next thing I noticed a few weeks ago in the shower was that some of my hair was gray at the ends but dark at the roots. So then I started counting dark vs. gray roots. When I had my hair colored for the wedding the hair dresser asked my age because I have a young face by I was more than 50% gray. Since I started counting, I noticed that 1/3 were gray and then 1/5 and then 1/7. Yesterday, out of the 69 hairs that fell out in the shower, 6 were gray. The rest were dark! So yes, I am vain enough that if not eating any wheat or dairy keeps my hair dark without coloring it and my nails healthy, AND the planet healthy...I can do this for the rest of my life. period. and resist temptations to cheat by having wheat or dairy "just this once..." So I'm happy. I'm healthy. I'm working on becoming so committed to being wheat and dairy free that I wouldn't even

CONSIDER ingesting any foods with wheat or dairy in them. And that's why I've announced to everyone that I'm wheat and dairy free from now on, to help me associate greater pain to breaking my decision to remain wheat and dairy free in the situations where it is the most tempting, hanging out with friends. I don't even really like the way wheat or dairy tastes and I REALLY don't like the way I feel when I eat them but I like to feel like I fit in and am not a freak. sigh. So we don't have wheat or dairy in the house. I'm not tempted to buy it when I'm out. When I'm with friends, I want to make sure that the social pressure to NOT eat food with wheat or dairy is so great that its easier NOT to eat it than to eat it.

10-08-2008

I have watched myself go from a person who doesn't exercise, to a person with a few extra curves, to a person who would rather put on a raincoat and bike in the rain than stay home because it feels so good to start my day with a bike ride. When I was a dancer, I was at the point where if I missed a day of stretching, I noticed, and I didn't miss a day because if I missed the morning workout for some reason, I would do it at night before going to sleep because to not do so felt wrong. And then I gradually stopped and got to the point where I didn't stretch or work out at all and then my size 8 pants were too tight and my size 10 pants were too tight, and eventually, the size 14 pants were uncomfortable, at which point I decided enough was enough and that it was time to take myself in hand. Today I realized I have shifted back to the other end of the pendulum. Yesterday, I felt like going for an evening bike ride because the weather was simply so gorgeous. I didn't go yesterday, but today I did. I notice my muscles thanking me as I use them and requesting that I use them now please if I delay my daily physical activity. I'm getting my flexibility back. I *love* feeling limber. I love seeing a well-defined shape when I look in the mirror. I don't feel like anything that Andrew and I are doing is hard. Yet many people are expressing surprise that we are doing everything at once and we have spent the better part of the last 13 months getting to this place. Why is it that now eating healthy foods and supplementing and pilates and cardio are so ingrained as a way of doing things that it's easier *to* do them than not, yet before the thought of doing everything every day was daunting? As soon as we wake up, *of course* we do our wealth conditioning exercises and meditations. They take minutes and make such a difference in setting the tone for the day. Yet there was a time when remembering to do it along with everything else was hard. It's like we've been building a plane. We got the engine and then the wings and the controls and the seats and it's like there was a blueprint in our heads of what this plane would look like and we started out with one piece, but then there were two and then four and the more pieces we had the more swooped in like there was this giant magnet or we turned on this attractive force and now when I look at what is assembling I can see it's a plane - it's not just "going to be" or something that exists only in my head. I can hear the motor starting to hum and I'm seeing more and more pieces fit together and we are preparing for take-off because there is the bone deep, unshakeable conviction that at any moment we will be in the air.

1-16-2009

I was thinking this morning that I've always felt that fanatics narrow minded, overly zealous, irrational idiots. And I guess the image of sprout eating, birkenstock wearing, co-op shopping people was a symbol for me of someone who was a fanatic, someone who was "waaay outthere" and someone who I did not want to be. And now I look at my life and I find myself reading books written in the late 60s and early 70s, directed to this audience (or trying to convince people to live from this perspective.) I am *completely* fanatical about my diet because to not be fanatic results in massive physical pain. "It's just one", or "live a little", or "it's Christmas", or "I don't want to offend so-and-so" don't work for me even a little and so I have been fanatical since last December with the results that I have energy, clear skin, stable moods and - oh yeah - am not wracked with debilitating pain and swelling that keeps me from doing normal activities like walking! I know the clincher for me was when the chiropractor convinced me to throw out my shoes and get some birkenstocks on the same day that I went to a pot luck and took a rice dish that I had read in a book that I had the ingredients for on hand that looked tasty. The ingredients were rice, tofu, tamari sauce and fresh mung bean sprouts. It was really good. But when I showed up and noticed that other people had brought things like store bought artichoke dip with dorritos, it really snapped into focus that the dish I brought was something I would think of as a stereotypical vegan fanatic's dish. It is probably what my aunt aurora was referring to when she told me she would never eat tofu. When I told her that the lasagna she had the last time she dined with us was made from tofu she replied, "Oh. Well I guess if you know how to cook it, then it's good." My mom was a fanatic for herself and her children but she didn't proselytize, though she had friends who did. I always felt sorry for their children because they all looked so sad and unhealthy. I want to be happy. I want to be healthy. I think a conversation with Andrew hit the nail on the head for me. "You're not a Food Nazi, you're discriminating!" He was asking me questions about my objections and what in particular it was that I didn't want to be like and he gave that group of people the name "Food Nazis." In Andrew's definition, a Food Nazi is someone who feels militantly about the way they eat for moral/environmental reasons. It's ok to read food nazi books for some of the good information they contain without agreeing with their militant stance. Andrew and I eat the way we eat because, as you said, it works well for us and to do otherwise would be BAD *for* US. He pointed out that when we have children who asks us why we eat what we do or why they can't eat x, y or the other we would explain to them that we work very hard to get them the food that works best for their particular set of genes and we spend considerable time and go to considerable effort to help them be the healthiest mostly highly functioning individuals you can be. When you are a grown up, feel free to make whatever choices you see fit. For now, this is what we're eating. He also pointed out that when they are teenagers, what they chose to eat is for the most part outside of our control and if the way they chose to rebel is by sneaking off to McDonalds with their friends, then we've done a pretty good job (he got this from conversations with my mother). He argued that if a Food Nazi's child asked similar questions they would get a rant about morality or the environment, etc. So realizing that I chose to eat, live, clothe myself the way I do because it *works* best *for* ME and not because I'm on a crusade to convince everyone else on the planet do the things I do, makes me feel a lot more relaxed about my life choices lately.

1-29-2009

I used to say that I was a vegetarian because my mom is vegan or because I prefer to eat foods that are still alive. I'm thinking I may shift more to the "anyone who isn't a vegetarian must not know about all the social, environmental and medical problems that meat consumption in general leads to!" response. I thought I was done with my meat-eaters rant but then this morning reading Tony Robbins book Awaken the Giant Within (see I have a source, it's no longer random people telling me stuff without any citations to back it up) he writes that 10% of US beef is imported from Central/South America and to support this demand rainforests are being cleared at the race of 1 acre/5 seconds. I've BEEN to Costa Rica. I've SEEN the cattle there. They ain't healthy. They don't look happy. I have never seen a cow in Costa Rica that was more than skin and bones and didn't have snot dripping out of its nose continuously. The rancher there tried to tell me it was just that variety of cow. Really? There is a variety of cow whose ribs show through its skin and has a river of mucus dripping down its nose when it's being fed what it needs and wants to be healthy? Could it perhaps be instead that COWS don't BELONG in a RAINFORREST????? Tony Robbins also writes that the amount of water used to raise one steer is enough to float an American destroyer. That's crazy!!! When I asked Andrew if he knew this he was like "yeah...the amount of water it takes to raise livestock is insane" and I'm thinking...with all the water shortages and water pollution issues..."WHY would ANYONE eat BEEF?" It's not just beef. According to Tony Robbin's book, 85% of topsoil loss is directly related to livestock production. "Every dollar that the government doles out to livestock producers in the form of irrigation subsidies actually costs taxpayers seven dollars in lost wages, higher cost of living and reduced business income." As if that weren't enough, if every American simply cut their meat intake by 10%, 100million people could be fed by the resources currently devoted to raising livestock that would be freed up by the reduction of demand. That's enough to feed all the starving people the world over AND have a surplus. No wonder there are militant vegetarians and vegans out there! It makes me less whiny about not eating cheese! Cause last time I checked, my favorite cheeses come from cows and let's not even get into the dairy industry...Well...at least this information is helping me form more references for dairy=BAD BAD BAD; dairy-free=SUPER GOOD for ME and the PLANET which I care about. In the past week from 2 different people I have heard that:

1/5 of CO_2 emissions world wide are a result of livestock production.

3/4 of all air and water pollution is tied to livestock.

In Iowa alone, hogs produce more than 50 million tons manure.

Meat consumption is linked to arthritis, cancer, heart disease, animal cruelty, food shortages.

2-10-2009

I *loved* the "pizza" at Cafe Gratitude. You see, pizza is one of those foods that I became addicted to. And then when I had to stop eating wheat, dairy, etc. I cried for 2 weeks and I cried if anyone ate pizza near me for the next 6 months. A year later, when someone made a pizza with a cornmeal crust and goat cheese, I decided to eat some. It was gross. I didn't like the textures or the way I felt afterward, even though it wasn't nearly as bad as I *used* to feel after eating pizza. So pizza was like this ephemeral food that represented everything I had given up, etc. At cafe gratitude, the crust is made from flax, the "cheese" is a cashew "ricotta" and it's topped with fresh pea shoots which give it exactly the freshness it needs. It was perfect! More than being delicious, it matches my mental idea of what pizza *should* taste like. It has all the pizza flavors I desire in the ratios I was seeking without the yuckiness that accompanies (for me) the food that most people think of as pizza. Does this make sense? I feel like I lost the food known as pizza twice. Once when I stopped eating it for health reasons and again a year later when I realized that the melted cheese on a bread is just so *gross* I don't ever *want* to eat it, even if I could. And at Cafe Gratitude, I found it again. And it was one of my *favorite* foods so it's like - not only was it good, it surpassed my expectations of anything food *could* be. And I felt *fantastic* after eating lunch *and* dessert there. Bonnie had a coconut cream pie made with coconuts and dates which was delicious. I had a nut milk vanilla ice cream sweetened with agave nectar which was *almost* as good as anything Andrew and I make, and certainly the best I've ever had in a restaurant.

3 BEST BREAKFASTS

ATOLE

My mother used to make us this cereal on cold winter days in New Mexico.

blue corn meal

water

salt, optional

Toast the blue corn meal over medium low heat. When it begins to smell fragrant, just after it changes color, but before it turns brown, add enough water to form a thin soup. Serve in a mug, adding salt, if desired.

CHAQUEWE

While my mother made this for us as well as atole, I remember my grandmother making it on occasion in the winter and we would eat it in front of the cast iron wood stove that was used to heat the breakfast nook at her house. I prefer atole, but I did admire the way the pat of butter my grandmother ate with her chaquewe would melt all over the bowl.

blue corn meal

water

salt, optional

red chili sauce, optional

Toast the blue corn meal over medium low heat. When it begins to smell fragrant, but before it changes color, add twice as much water as blue corn meal, adding salt, if desired. Stir constantly to dispel all lumps. It will form a thick porridge. Serve hot! After serving, add red chili sauce if desired.

ANDREW'S OATMEL

This is Andrew's recipe for oatmeal because he doesn't like guesswork and it produces a consistency he adores every time. Serves 3

1 ½ cup oats

3 cups water

Put the oats and water in a sauce pot over medium low heat. If desired a higher heat can be used if the porridge is stirred constantly to avoid sticking and burning. When the oats are cooked, serve with maple syrup or soy milk, vanilla and agave nectar to taste.

SPICY APPLESAUCE

10 apples

1 ½ teaspoon cinnamon

½ teaspoon powdered ginger root

water

Cut the apples into halves and remove the stems and seeds. Place them in a large stock pot. Add the spices and enough water to cover half the apples. Bring the water to a boil. Cover tightly and reduce to a simmer. When the apples are tender, put them through a food mill or mash them by hand.

PANCAKES

PLOYES

French Acadian Buckwheat Pancakes. I first tasted these at a celebration of a local natural food store. They were demonstrating a mix and I decided to purchase the mix and then experiment at home. The following recipe is what I came up with and they are delicious!

Sift

1 cup buckwheat flour

1 cup flour

4 teaspoons baking powder

½ teaspoon salt

Add

2 2/3 cups water

Let the batter rest while heating an ungreased skillet to 400 degrees. You will notice as you are cooking them that if the temperature is too low, they will stick to the griddle. If it is too high, they will burn before cooking through. Spoon 1-3 tablespoons of batter onto the hot skillet, using a spoon to spread it to 1/8 inch thick. Most recipes say to cook on one side only, but it works equally well to flip them. Serve as you would crepes.

SCONES

THYME SCONES

One day I wanted biscuits, but didn't have my mother's recipe so I decided to take my scone recipe, omit the sugar and use savory herbs instead of fruit. It worked! And we have been enjoying them ever since. For plain biscuits, simply omit the thyme.

2 cups whole wheat pastry flour

2 teaspoons non-aluminum baking powder

½ teaspoon sea salt

4 tablespoons coconut oil

¾-1 cup water

3-5 sprigs of fresh thyme

What to do:

Mix the dry ingredients. Rub in the fat with a pastry cutter or two butter knives. add fresh thyme leaves. Add the water. Spoon onto a cooking sheet and bake for approximately 10 minutes in an oven preheated to 425.

ALMOND GRAPE SOUP

In Spain, there is a soup made with almonds and green grapes. Unfortunately, the Spanish version also has garlic and sherry. Nevertheless, I was intrigued and one morning, I enjoyed this delightful soup for breakfast. Don't pair it with anything other than semi-acidic fruits to take fun advantage of the all the nutrients this soup provides.

½ pound raw almonds
1 pound strawberries, hulled
1 bunch green grapes
apple juice

Blend almonds, followed by the strawberries. Add enough apple juice to barely cover the almonds. Blend to a coarse puree and add the grapes, a few at a time. Serve this beautifully chunky, pink soup in 4 white bowls.

FRUIT SOUP

There is a cookbook dedicated to preschoolers titled "Pretend Soup and Other Real Recipes." All their recipes call for dairy or eggs or both, but their idea of "Pretend Soup" intrigued me. Essentially, they poured juice in a bowl and then added chopped fruit. It seemed like something that everyone, not just preschoolers could enjoy. The following combinations are yummy:

apple juice, strawberries, ground almonds;
apple juice, strawberries, blueberries, ripe banana;
apple juice, strawberries, raspberries, ripe banana;
apple juice, wild blueberries, raspberries, strawberries, ground almonds
apple juice, strawberries, peaches, cherries;
apple juice, white grape juice, peaches, strawberries;
apple juice, banana, strawberries, mangoes, peaches, blueberries;
coconut-pineapple juice, raspberries;
purple grape juice, pineapple, green grapes;
purple grape juice, wild blueberries, raspberries;
orange juice, strawberries;
orange juice, blueberries;
orange juice, ground almonds, honey;
lemonade, frozen cherries;

SALAD SOUP

This soup is great to make in the morning and drink not only for breakfast, but also throughout the day whenever you feel hungry.

green leek tops, well washed

celery stalks, well washed

parsley greens, gently washed

romaine lettuce, mixed baby greens, spinach, alfalfa sprouts – whatever you have on hand that is green

filtered water

salt and lemon

Put salt and greens in a stock pot with water, then bring to a boil. Reduce to a simmer until the greens float to the bottom. Serve with a squeeze of fresh lemon in each bowl. - Good for a general spring cleanse.

SMOOTHIES

The spring and summer months are the perfect time to enjoy blended drinks, also known as "smoothies!" My mother and Andrew both prefer very smooth evenly textured smoothies. I prefer smoothies with some crunch to them. Consequently, I will frequently toss in almonds if I am making the smoothie for myself or myself and Elena and only pulse it for a few seconds – just enough that the almonds are roughly chopped. Andrew never puts nuts in any of the smoothies he makes and my mother puts almonds in the blender and pulverizes them into flour and then adds the fruits and juices. The combinations and amounts can be varied with lovely results depending on season and individual taste.

orange juice, almonds and honey;

apple juice, frozen strawberries, almonds;

apple juice, frozen strawberries, frozen blueberries, ripe banana;

fresh pineapple and purple grape juice;

coconut milk, pineapple juice, frozen raspberries;

apple juice, frozen strawberries, frozen raspberries, ripe banana;

orange juice, ripe banana, frozen strawberries;

orange juice, ripe banana, frozen blueberries;

purple grape juice, wild blueberries, frozen raspberries

wild blueberries, raspberries, strawberries, almonds

lemonade, frozen cherries;

apple juice, frozen strawberries, frozen peaches, frozen cherries;

apple juice, white grape juice, frozen peaches, fresh strawberries;

apple juice, banana, frozen strawberries, frozen mangoes, frozen peaches, frozen blueberries;

almonds, frozen cranberries, pear

almonds, fresh cranberries, apple

4 SALADS, SIDES AND OTHER ACCOMPANIMENTS

DRESSINGS

BASIC DRESSING
lemon juice
salt
dried herbs such as oregano or basil
Plate your salad or vegetables to be dressed. Add a squeeze of fresh lemon, a dash of salt or herbs, and enjoy.

PESTO DRESSING
1 bunch basil
¼ teaspoon salt
10 stems of parsley
2/3 cup sunflower seeds
a generous handful of arugula
juice from one lemon
Finely grind the sunflower seeds and salt in a blender. Add lemon juice and parsley. Add basil and arugula. Transfer immediately to a glass container. Cover with olive oil. Refrigerate until using. When using for a salad, put a ½ cup of dressing in the bottom of a medium serving bowl. Add olive oil and additional lemon juice if desired. When well mixed, add the rest of the salad. Toss and serve.

TAHINI DRESSING
Elena's favorite dressing of all time...
1 heaping tablespoon tahini
juice from one lemon
salt
olive oil, optional
pesto, optional
crushed tomatoes, optional

Put a tablespoon or so of tahini in the bottom of your salad bowl. Add a sprinkle of salt and enough lemon juice to the tahini so that it changes consistency. If the lemons are especially tart I may add some olive oil. For variation, I sometimes add pesto or crushed tomatoes at this stage. Add the remaining salad ingredients to the bowl and serve immediately.

FAUX DAIRY

FRESH "CHEESE"
raw macadamia nuts (roughly 2 cups)
filtered water
1 clove garlic
olive oil to taste
Soak the macadamia nuts for at least 4 hours, or overnight. Combine soaked nuts, garlic, and olive oil in a food processor with the s blade attachment. Shape into "slices."

CASHEW CHEESE
3 cups raw cashews
filtered water
4 tablespoons lemon juice
½ teaspoon salt
¾ cup fresh water
Soak cashews for 8 hours in filtered water. After soaking, rinse them and put them in a food processor with lemon juice, salt and ¾ cup fresh water. Be prepared to add as much as an additional ¾ cup water to the cashew mixture to achieve the desired consistency.

BRAZIL NUT "PARMESAN" CHEESE
raw brazil nuts (roughly 2 cups)
¼ teaspoon of salt
a clove of garlic (optional)
Combine all ingredients in the food processor with s blade attachment.

TOFU "RICOTTA" CHEESE
1 pound extra firm tofu
basil to taste
salt to taste
olive oil to taste
water
Put the tofu in the blender with the basil, salt and olive oil. My favorite proportions are roughly 2 tablespoons basil, ½ teaspoon salt and roughly 3 tablespoons olive oil. I add more or less (as little as ½ or a much as 2 cups) a cup of water and then spoon the cheese into my lasagna or eggplant manicotti before baking.

SALADS

I realize I am not a salad person. I don't live for salads. I particularly dislike taking the time to prep the ingredients whether that is collecting/washing greens, making the dressing, or chopping things up. That being said the salads here are salads which were delicious and memorable enough to be worth the effort to make and eat over and over again.

Unless otherwise specified, the directions for each salad dish is simply to toss together and serve! You may wish to rip lettuces into bite sized pieces. You may choose to serve larger pieces on a salad plate with a knife and fork. The presentation is entirely up to you and is an opportunity to let your imagination run riot!

ANDREW'S SALAD
When we were living in Menlo Park, Andrew would make this salad for lunch on a fairly regular basis. This was a great surprise to his mother because it contains both nuts and olives, two foods he eschewed vigorously before marrying me.

romaine lettuce
sun dried tomatoes
black olives
brazil nut "parmesan cheese"

BLACK BEAN CORN SALAD
This salad is particularly delicious in the summer when fresh corn is in season. In fact, the first time I had it was at a vegan bar-b-que, the only bar-b-que I have ever been to where I was able to eat more than soda and chips.

black beans, cooked
fresh corn, removed from cob
avocado, chopped
fresh tomatoes, chopped
salt, optional
olive oil, optional
lime juice, optional

MOROCCAN CARROT SALAD

I found variations of this salad in every Moroccan cookbook I've ever read. Below are the proportions I prefer.

1 stem of green garlic, minced
roughly one pound of carrots, grated
3 tablespoons olive oil
juice from one lemon
½ teaspoon salt
1 teaspoon ground cumin

In a saute pan, place olive oil, garlic, cumin and salt. Put it over medium high heat. When the cumin is infused throughout the oil, add the carrots. Cook until the garlic is wilted. Remove from heat and serve, or let cool and serve with lemon juice.

CUCUMBER SALAD

This salad showcases the best of summer ingredients. It has parsley which is good for protecting against sunburn and make a beautiful accompaniment to hummus, pita, tabouli or falafel.

2 tomatoes, chopped
1 cucumber, chopped
1 green pepper, chopped
6 sprigs of fresh parsley, chopped
3 tablespoons olive oil
juice from one lemon
½ teaspoon salt
¼ cup tahini (optional)

Mix salt, tahini and lemon juice. When they are well combined, toss in the remaining ingredients and serve immediately.

DINNER SALAD

This simple salad is an elegant addition to a dinner party or romantic meal.

1 head lettuce
1 organic rose
dried basil
dried oregano
garnishing salt
olive oil
lemon juice

Toss everything except the rose together just before serving. Place the rose in the center as a garnish or scatter a few rose petals on each salad place or over the top of the dressed salad.

FAVORITE FRUIT SALAD

A neighbor brought this salad to a summer block party in New England. It is appealing both texturally and visually, as well as being a fantastic combination of flavors. Thank you, Cindy Grace!

fresh strawberries
fresh Blueberries
fresh Raspberries
fresh Blackberries
unsweetened canned pineapple chunks
unsweetened coconut flakes

FENNEL SALAD

When I was pregnant with my first child, I had a lot of trouble finding something to eat. This salad was reliably delicious and is also enjoyable when I'm not pregnant!

fennel bulb, sliced
safflower oil
salt
celery seeds
mesclun greens
pumpkin seeds

Saute the fennel bulb in safflower oil with celery seeds and salt. Toss over mesclun greens. Top with pumpkin seeds. A complete protein and filling lunch.

GREEK SALAD

My sister Aja went to New York to be a runway model. While in New York, she met a music producer whose family was from Greece. When she came home to visit, she made this salad for us as an accompaniment to every lunch and dinner. It's a perfect quick, simple, salad.

4-6 leaves red romaine lettuce
a few shavings (translucently thin slices) of red onion
sea salt
lemon juice
olive oil
dried basil
dried greek oregano

GREEN GODDESS SALAD

This became my very favorite summer salad to make and I made it fresh every day one summer for as long as I could get my hands on zebra tomatoes and cucumber. I created it initially because I wanted to make my Jordanian Salad, but was out of salt. I reasoned that a little pesto would cure the lack of salt and boy did it ever! I was delighted by the visual appeal of green salad vegetables with green dressing and the taste was so heavenly, I had to call this the green goddess salad!

½ head of lettuce
½ cucumber
2 green zebra tomatoes
1 heaping tablespoon tahini
lemon juice to taste
olive oil to taste
several tablespoons "best pesto evar" (sunflower seed version)

In a small bowl, combine the tahini, lemon juice and olive oil until a nice homogeneous paste is formed. Roughly chop the tomatoes and cucumber and add them. Stirring thoroughly so that each chunk is well coated. Add the pesto and mix well. Wash the lettuce, tear it into bite sized bits and arrange it on a plate so the stems form the bottom layer and the thin leafy bits are on top. Spoon the cucumber, tomato mixture over the lettuce and enjoy! Mmm...

HOUSE SALAD

1 leaf of red leaf lettuce per person
sliced cucumber
sliced tomato
sliced onion
lemon juice
olive oil
salt
basil and or oregano

JORDANIAN SALAD

The first time Andrew and I went out was for a casual lunch at a restaurant that had the virtue of being open and nearby. I didn't know a falafel from a dolma, so we ordered many small dishes. The majority of the dishes are lost in the mists of time, but my favorite, called "Jordanian Salad" was identical to the "Israeli Salad" save for the addition of tahini. I have no idea exactly how they made that salad or even if either salad is authentic, but whenever I make this salad, I think of that day.

tomatoes, roughly chopped
cucumber, roughly chopped
green pepper, cubed
olive oil (roughly 1/3 cup)
lemon juice (roughly 1/3 cup)
½ teaspoon salt
tahini (roughly 1/3 cup)
small tomato

Combine tahini, lemon juice, olive oil and salt until creamy. Chop a small tomato with all it's juices over the mixture and mix tomato juice, seeds and pulp throughout the dressing. Add the cubed pepper, roughly chopped tomatoes and cucumber. Stir so that each piece of salad is liberally coated with dressing and serve immediately.

KALE SALAD

I am not a fan of kale in general and raw kale in particular. I was dismayed to find it seemed to be one of the only healthy foods available in winter in New England. One of the first friends we made when we moved to the East Coast loves kale and puts it in almost everything. I have enjoyed every kale dish she has ever prepared, but this salad is so delicious, I begged her for the recipe and she is sure to make it for me whenever the opportunity presents itself.

Juice of 1 lemon (substitute big splash of apple cider vinegar in a pinch)

Big splash of extra virgin olive oil (optional)

Small splash of toasted pumpkin seed oil (substitute balsamic vinegar in a pinch)

1 tsp. Celtic or other sea salt

1 bunch curly kale, thinly shredded

1 small red onion or large shallot, halved & sliced paper-thin

1-2 medium carrots, grated

1 avocado, cut into small chunks

Gently stir liquid ingredients and salt in bottom of large bowl (one with a lid). Clean and dry kale, or prepare first and use a salad spinner afterward. Cut stems off kale and compost. If kale is large and fibrous, remove large vein in middle of each leaf, as well. Then stack several leaves and slice as thinly as possible: you want to maximize surface area so that the marinade can soften the kale as much as possible. Add onion, carrot, and avocado. Mix well. Cover tightly, and refrigerate. Let sit at least 2 hours. Ideal at 4-6 hours old. Keeps well for 3 days.

MARINATED TOFU SALAD

I was reading the book, Not Eating Out in NYC and while the author was describing a chicken dish, I wondered what the results would be if I put together the following recipe. The results are well worth repeating!

extra firm tofu cut into 1/4"x1/2"x1"pieces

1/3 cup apple cider vinegar

1/3 cup sesame oil

1/3 cup tamari sauce

1 bunch fresh basil, chopped

1 bunch arugula, chopped

Marinate the tofu in vinegar, sesame oil and tamari sauce for about an hour. Then and the basil and arugula. Serve with a nice slice of bread or 3 teaspoons of cooked quinoa to absorb the excess juice.

MESCLUN SALAD
salad greens
olive oil
herbs
sea salt

Gently toss washed and dried mesclun salad greens with olive oil and dried herbs and sea salt. A tablespoon of dried basil and a teaspoon of dried oregano or thyme are typical, but herbs de provence, or any combination of fresh or dried herbs that you find pleasing work well.

MILLET SALAD

I wanted to make a wheat free tabouli salad for my friends as they prepared for the baby shower they were throwing me. Someone thought it was done before I added the lemon juice and salt. So we served both salads side by side and enjoyed both!

1 cup millet, cooked
1 bell pepper, finely chopped
parsley, chopped
olive oil to taste

After cooking the millet in salt water, toss it with the bell pepper, parsley and olive oil. Enjoy warm or cold.

MILLET SALAD VARIATION

I made this the morning of the baby shower my friends threw me so that we would have something filling and nutritious to eat while getting ready for all the guests. I was thinking of tabouli salad at the time, but I can't eat wheat and thought cooked millet might be a good substitute. It was.

1 cup millet, cooked
1 bell pepper, finely chopped
parsley, chopped
olive oil to taste
lemon juice
salt

After cooking the millet in salt water, toss it with remaining ingredients. Enjoy warm or cold.

MOZZARELLA ALA CAPRESE SALAD

This is probably my husband's favorite salad of all time.

Fresh cheese, sliced

Organic heirloom tomatoes, sliced

Large leaves of fresh basil

Olive oil

Roasted red peppers (optional)

This salad is perfect when served with a garden salad for lunch on a spring or summer day. Since it calls for cheese, make sure you do not eat it within 3 hours of eating carbohydrates, melons or fruits. It goes well with slices of cucumber.

NORTHERN CALIFORNIA SPRING SALAD

Everyone knows I dislike beets. As a kid, I appreciated a pinch of beet water (water left over from steaming beets for my Dad) in my mashed potatoes because it turned them hot pink! But everyone knew that my Dad was the only one who liked beets because beets are gross. As an adult, I met a friend for lunch at a very exclusive restaurant in Northern California and the *only* item on the menu that wasn't pre-made was their salad. Their salad had various cheeses and meats and also called for mache, but they were able to make a version that I could eat and it naturally came with beets because if we removed the beets in addition to all the meats and cheeses, there wasn't really a whole lot left to the salad. To my utmost surprise, I enjoyed my salad so much so, that when I saw some baby beets for sale at the farmer's market, I bought them and roasted the roots, letting my husband use the beet tops in one of his delicious stir fries. The following salad is what we made that afternoon and it was so good it eclipsed all memories of the original salad that inspired it. This salad is now my favorite way of consuming beets. Moreover, I have been known to buy beets on more than one occasion specifically to be able to make this salad!

Cooked Beets

Fennel

Asparagus

lemon

sesame oil

sea salt or brazil nut "parmesan cheese"

Layer the beets on the bottom of a white plate (I like the color contrast). Cut the feathery part of the fennel away from the stalk and set it aside. Slice the stalk thinly as though it were an onion and lightly saute it in sesame oil. Lightly steam the asparagus (less than 3 minutes). If you are using salt instead of brazil nuts, add the salt to the sauteed fennel stalk and then use it to form the second layer of the salad. Chop the feathery bits of the fennel and use this (raw) as the third layer of the salad. The steam from the cooked fennel stalks and beets will make this just tender enough. Cover with freshly steamed asparagus. Drizzle with sesame oil. Top with lemon and brazil nuts.

TUMERIA'S PASTA SALAD

Tumeria brought this pasta salad to a vegan bar-b-que one summer. Bar-b-ques for me are typically a bunch of people I don't know, or don't know well, sitting around eating totally disgusting foods, inviting me to join in consuming things that either make me super sick, are totally gross or are both. I usually choose between eating before I go or eating the one thing I've brought. Either way, I feel like an odd duck. I don't seem to give off the "I love bar-b-que" vibe to people who know me well. The vegan bar-b-que where I encountered this salad, was a completely different experience. Instead of going to watch a bunch of strangers, or near strangers eat really disgusting foods that I wouldn't put near my mouth in a million years and feeling completely inept, socially, we had a delightful visit with utterly charming people. I loved that everyone labeled (down to the brand of oil) what ingredients they used in each dish they brought or brought the packaging for others to inspect and determine if it was something they wanted to consume or not. I love that nothing had a disgusting nasty dressing on it and everything tasted as good (or in the case of this pasta salad - better!) as it looked. I appreciated that people talked about where to find yummy groceries, how to grow food organically, what restaurants were good and which were terrible for vegans, what to do to increase the amount of trash being recycled at the city level and where to buy the best shoes! There were 5 people there who we had met before and we made plans to hang out again soon. The rest of the crowd were friends we just hadn't met yet! The weather was around 70 degrees with a clear blue sky and the bar-b-que was free of bugs and other. For the first time in my life, I could see the appeal of a bar-b-que. It's easy! There is little to clean both before or after. All in all, I couldn't imagine a more perfect experience of a summer afternoon. It was too hot to make any of the dishes we traditionally take to potlucks so we took blue corn chips and number 9 salsa. The hosts provided seitan steaks (which Andrew enjoyed), vegan sausage (which Bonnie adored), grilled veggies, corn on the cob, baked potatoes, non-gross veggie burgers and plates/utensils. They asked guests to bring side dishes. I was glad we brought chips and salsa because someone else brought guacamole, but forgot chips. Someone else brought a large bowl of organic lettuce and someone brought a heaping platter of brandy wine tomatoes from their garden. The most surprising dish. It was not surprising to see a pasta salad. It was surprising that I could eat it and, even more surprising, that I enjoyed it! It was delicious and also the first pasta salad I have ever had that wasn't the most disgusting thing ever! We simply had to acquire the recipe. Mix it all up and there you have it!

brown rice pasta, cooked
finely chopped onion
finely chopped celery
finely chopped red pepper
1 can red kidney beans
Veganaise and pickle relish to taste

SPRING LUNCH SALAD
Organic baby greens
cheese or toasted walnuts
red onions, thinly sliced
sauteed baby mushrooms
lemon juice

SUMMER SALAD
fresh tomatoes, sliced in ½
cucumbers, thinly slices
bell peppers, sliced into rings
fresh basil leaves and parsley
macadamia nut cheese (optional)
lemon juice, olive oil and salt
olives

The cheese and olives should be added just before serving but the other ingredients may be combined several hours before serving and allowed to marinate.

SUMMER GARDEN SALAD
4-6 leaves red romaine lettuce
2 full or 5 small springs small leaf basil
7-10 dandelion leaves*
1 red bell pepper or ½ sliced cucumber.

The dandelion leaves should be harvested from an area where no pesticides have been used that is also away from cars. The leaves should be no larger than your pinky finger in length or width, otherwise they will be bitter.

SAUCES AND SPICES

BROWN SAUCE

This came together quite by accident one day when I started to follow a new recipe for Pad Thai, got distracted and stopped half way through. It works well for pouring over rice and vegetables or for throwing into a quick stir fry.

2/3 cup boiling water
1 tablespoon tamarind concentrate
2 tablespoons sesame oil
3 tablespoons tamari sauce
3 tablespoons agave nectar

Dissolve tamarind concentrate in boiling water. Then add remaining ingredients.

THE BEST EVAR!!!

There have been pestos I've enjoyed and pestos I really haven't cared for. One summer in CA, we had so much basil, I was making pesto on a regular basis. When I made the recipe below, it was so delightful I wrote down what I had just done and have been making reliably delicious pesto every since!

1 bunch basil
½ teaspoon salt
2 med cloves garlic
10-20 stems of parsley
approximately 2/3 cup pine nuts
a generous handful of arugula
olive oil

Pulse garlic in the food processor with salt. This insures the garlic is minced and the salt evenly distributed so you don't end up with one bite that has too much garlic or too much salt. Add parsley next. The parsley gives this a beautiful green color. Add pine nuts. If you add them too early, it will be hard to make sure everything is smoothly incorporated and no one likes to find a mouthful of parsley stem, garlic or salt. Add alternate handfuls of basil and arugula. Transfer immediately to a glass container. Seal the top with olive oil immediately to prevent the basil from oxidizing and turning black. I frequently cover mine with up to an inch or so of olive oil replacing the olive oil as I use it so that the top layer is always protected from air. refrigerate until using.

GARAHM MASALA

They say there are as many recipes for garahm masala as there are cooks who use it. This is my favorite recipe because I came up with it myself. A friend of mine made garahm masala ice cream and my sister observed it tasted like the eggnog we loved. Shortly afterward, I saw a commercial preparation of garahm masala that called for the spices listed below and so I began experimenting until I came up with a combination that tasted like I remembered our favorite eggnog tasting! I have since used it in bharta, butternut squash soup, pumpkin pie...I have so many uses for garahm masala, I always keep some on hand.

1/8 teaspoon cloves
¼ teaspoon cardamom
1 teaspoon cinnamon
1 whole nutmeg, grated

GREEN CHILI

Wash peppers, checking each one to make sure it is firm, not mushy or withered. Heat cast iron skillet to high. This works best on a pan devoted solely to the purpose of roasting peppers or making tortillas. Place peppers on hot griddle and let them rest until the skin begins to char. Turn each pepper so that the skin is charred evenly. If you don't leave it long enough, the skin will stick. If you leave it to long, the meat under the skin will burn. When the pepper is blackened on all sides, put it in a bowl with a tight fitting lid to let it sweat. After sweating, the pepper can be peeled and eaten, or wrapped in a freezer proof container and frozen with it's peel intact for later use. To use frozen peppers, run pepper briefly under water and then remove the skin before consuming.

GREEN GARLIC

My favorite thing is to make a meal of things from my garden. One spring favorite involves roasting root vegetables with rosemary, olive oil and green garlic. I like to serve it with garlic bread and a side dish of broccoli or asparagus lightly steamed with a lemon olive oil sauce. Green garlic was something I was unfamiliar with until joining Community Supported Agriculture in Northern California. When green garlic came in our CSA box one week, I used it as I would green onions and thoroughly enjoyed its delicate flavor. I forgot about it until one day early this spring, I wanted to make garlic bread and realized I had planted the cloves of garlic that had been hanging around the kitchen. There around the rose bush, thin little stems of green garlic had pushed their way up through the snow. No sooner could you say "One, two, three..." than I had four little baby garlic stems in my hand. I brought them in and washed them. Some I chopped for the potatoes I was about to roast and some I sauteed with oil to make garlic bread.

GREEN GARLIC STIR FRY

Green garlic has a more delicate flavor than dried garlic does. It appears at growers markets and in health food stores in the fall and in the spring. It can also be grown by planting a clove of garlic (unpeeled, pointing part towards the sky) at any time of year, and looking for garlic shoots in fall and spring. Garlic cloves planted in a circle around rose bushes keep aphids and other yucky bugs away. Garlic and roses like the same amount of watering since both grow in stream banks in their natural habitat.

2 tablespoons sunflower oil
1 red onion, chopped
2 tablespoons red chili powder
1 ½ tablespoons powdered ginger
¼ cup tamari sauce
¼ cup sesame seeds
1 pound firm tofu, cubed
baby bok choi
asparagus
green beans
broccoli
sugar snap peas
bean sprouts
mushrooms
green garlic, chopped
fresh parsley, chopped

Heat the oil in a large cast iron skillet. When it is hot, add the onions. When the onions start to cook, add the chili, ginger, tamari sauce and tofu. When the tofu has absorbed the sauce, begin adding the vegetables one at a time beginning with the garlic and then moving from most hardy to most delicate. Any combination of the vegetables listed above will be delicious. In the above list I would add first green beans, then broccoli, asparagus, mushrooms, baby bok choi, sugar snap peas, bean sprouts, parsley, sesame seeds. Serve immediately.

FRESH HERB MIX
One sprig fresh rosemary
One carrot top
3-4 shoots of green garlic (stems 1/8 or smaller in diameter)

ANDREW'S MARINARA SAUCE

To my surprise, Andrew's marinara does not have dried basil. He uses crushed tomatoes canned with basil, but doesn't add additional dried basil.

1 large onion

crushed tomatoes with basil

salt to taste

red chili powder to taste, (less than ¼ teaspoon)

oregano to taste

thyme or fresh chopped rosemary, optional

oil

Mince the onion. Add oil to a sauce pan. When the oil is warm, add the onions. Let the onions soften with the salt and herbs. When the onions are caramelized, add tomatoes. Use with pasta, as the red sauce in lasagna, eggplant manicotti or pizza.

BASIC MARINARA SAUCE

oil (about 2 tablespoons)

an onion

tomatoes (3 - 4 cups chopped or crushed)

oregano (½ - 1 teaspoon)

basil (twice as much as oregano)

salt (½ – 1 teaspoon)

Heat oil in a medium sauce pan. Saute onion. Add tomatoes and herbs and salt to taste.

BASIC TOMATO PASTE SAUCE

oil

onion

tomato paste

water

basil

oregano

salt

Heat 2 tablespoons oil. Saute an onion. Add tomato paste and enough water to achieve the desired consistency of tomato sauce. Add dried basil, dried oregano and salt.

BASIC MARINARA VEGETABLE VARIANTS
oil (about 2 tablespoons)
an onion
bell pepper
mushrooms
eggplant
spinach
tomatoes (3 - 4 cups chopped or crushed)
oregano (½ - 1 teaspoon)
basil (twice as much as oregano)
salt (½ – 1 teaspoon)

Heat oil in a medium sauce pan. Saute onion. Add bell pepper, mushrooms or eggplant. When they are tender, add spinach, if using and tomatoes. Add herbs and salt to taste.

MARINARA HERB VARIANTS
Use chopped fresh rosemary instead of oregano; Use fresh oregano and rosemary; Add fresh basil leaves, chopped as a topping over the pasta after it is served.

RED CHILI POWDER
Use red chili powder measure for measure instead of black pepper.

For example, instead of putting salt and pepper on your soup, put salt and red chili powder; instead of salt and pepper in mashed potatoes, put salt and red chili powder.

RED CHILI SAUCE
Make a red chili sauce. Put red chili powder and flour in a dry skillet. Turn the heat on high and stir constantly. When the smell of the chili and toasting flour fills the kitchen but before it begins to darken, transfer to a sauce pan with 2 tablespoons oil and add water. Cook the sauce over medium heat (warm enough to form little bubbles, cool enough not to be a roiling boil) stirring constantly (to prevent formation of lumps) until the sauce begins to thicken. If the sauce is beginning to thicken and there are still some lumps, you can pour it into a blender and buzz it a few times to get the lumps out. Add salt to taste before pouring the sauce over anything. The ratio of chili powder to flour will affect the heat of the finished sauce. To start out I use 4 tablespoons red chili, 4 tablespoons flour, 4 cups water, 2 tablespoons sunflower oil, 1 teaspoon salt. If the sauce is too hot, the next time I will use 2 tablespoons chili and 6 tablespoons flour. If it is not hot enough I might use 6 tablespoons red chili powder and 2 tablespoons flour.

The gluten in the flour is what causes the sauce to thicken.

DUSHENKA'S NOT- HOT SALSA

I came up with this when I first started dating my now husband who was born on Long Island, NY and completely unaccustomed to any food with any hint of heat. I wanted to enjoy chips and salsa with him and this recipe works.

1 can whole peeled tomatoes with basil

juice from 1 lemon

4-7 sprigs parsley; 2 sprigs small leaf basil

3 green onions

Salt to taste. Chop herbs and onions finely. Mix all ingredients in a medium sized bowl. Enjoy with tortilla chips.

SALSA FRESCA

I am not a fan of cilantro. And, occasionally I am hungry for a salsa fresca I ate once at a friends house that included cilantro.

chopped tomatoes

chopped green onion

chopped hot pepper

lemon juice

salt to taste

1 can whole peeled tomatoes

RANCHOS SALSA

In San Diego there is a vegan organic mexican restaurant called Ranchos. My mother took me there when my sister moved there in February and I was so enamored with their food that my sister would call me and ask when I was coming back for a visit because she was feeling hungry for Ranchos. When I went to San Diego for my brother's wedding, I realized that my beans are better, my potatoes are better, my calabacitas are better, my tamales and enchiladas are infinitely better... In fact, I like everything they serve better when I make it in my own kitchen with the exception of their salsa. Their salsa is the best salsa I've ever had, and being raised in New Mexico, I have eaten quite a bit of salsa in my day. When I returned to New England from my brother's wedding, I was already missing Ranchos salsa on the plane ride home. Luckily for me, I returned during a glut of fresh ripe tomatoes and perfect pepper and abundant onions. All of this led me to recreating Rancho's salsa, or at least, a salsa that is exactly what I want to eat when I want salsa.

ripe tomatoes (several large)
green onions (scallions)
green raw annaheim pepper
lemon juice
salt

Put all the vegetables in the blender and liquify them. Add lemon juice and salt to taste. When I first did this, hoping to recreate Ranchos salsa, I was disappointed that instead of the salsa I was hoping for, what I created was a spicy v-8 or bloody mary mix. Yuck! Luckily I needed to go do something else and decided to toss it into a mason jar and refrigerate it until I could figure out what to do with it. The next day, I realized the "juice" had separated in the pulpy part (which looked and tasted like what they serve at Ranchos for salsa) and a clear liquid. I don't know how long this keeps in the fridge as the longest mine has lasted is a week – and that was when I started out with 8 cups. Yes, that was a lot of tomatoes.

TOMATO "CREME" SAUCE
Perfect for raw food dishes.
2 cups sunflower seeds
1 jar sun dried tomatoes packed in olive oil
water

Put sunflower seeds the food processor with a jar of sun dried tomatoes and pulse until a paste is achieved. Add enough water to achieve the consistency of a tomato creme sauce.

TZADZIKI SAUCE
vegan mayonnaise
dill
parsley (optional)
garlic (optional)
onion (optional)
What to do: chop all the ingredients finely (I put them all in the food processor and about 10 seconds later it's done) and then stir them into the vegan mayonnaise If I am just adding dill to veganaise, there is no need to involve a food processor. A simple spoon will suffice.

ZA'ATAR
2 parts ground sumac
2 parts dried thyme
1 part sesame seeds

SIDES

ALOO SAAG
Aloo saag is one of my favorite dishes, and the dish made famous in Andrew's tales of our first date. When I nailed the recipe for Aloo saag, I did a happy dance.
Heat a large sauce pan and add oil. When the oil is hot, add
¾ teapoon of cumin seeds
1 teaspoon of ground turmeric
¼ teaspoon of ground chili powder
When you smell the spices, add a
chopped onion
and let the onion cook in the oil and spices. When the oil is cooked, add
300g baby spinach leaves
300g baby kale leaves
Put in one handful at a time and let it wilt before adding the next handful and stirring. When all the greens are wilted. put everything, including the liquid that may have left the greens in a blender to puree. In the meantime, put
5 tablespoons of fat or oil in a large pan over medium heat. When the oil is hot, add
¾ teaspoons of garahm masala
Then add cooked potatoes or cubed tofu, if using, and when they are coated with the oil and garahm masala, add the spinach mixture. Thoroughly combine, and then serve.

ALOO TIKKI

When Nalini made me aloo paratha, she also made aloo tikki. Her recipe is below, but when she made it that night, she used the filling from aloo paratha, adding enough chickpea flour that we could shape it into patties and followed the directions below for cooking the patties.

chickpea flour
½ teaspoon salt
coriander leaves
diced green chili
3-4 potatoes
cumin powder
lemon juice
chili powder
salt
grated ginger

Boil potatoes. Remove from water and mash. Mix with remaining ingredients and form into patties. Brush oil on both sides and cook on the flat griddle. Flip over when bottom is cooked and cook it on the other side. Serve hot.

APPLE FACES

I remember first eating these at a Halloween party in my second grade classroom.

apples
peanut butter
raisins

Core each apple and slice in ½. Spread each half with peanut butter and decorate with raisins.

ASPARAGUS

Asparagus is a lovely vegetable that I like best lightly steamed. I have an asparagus pot, a lovely addition to my kitchen, but by no means, necessary. Choose asparagus that are firm, green and not withered. I like the thinner stalks best. To steam the asparagus, rinse the bunch in a bowl of filtered water, being careful not to leave the asparagus in the water so that the water soluble vitamins and minerals are retained. Snap each stalk at the bottom before steaming and they will break just where they become tough. Save the bottoms for soup or soup stock. When you have snapped off the ends, put the asparagus in a steamer, or the basket of your asparagus pot with just enough filtered water that the asparagus is not in water. Put the pot over high heat and, shortly, the asparagus will be bright green and ready to eat!

Save the water for a soup, or drink it as a healthful asparagus infusion. In roman times there was an expression "In as little time as it takes to cook asparagus..." meaning "very quickly."

ASPARAGUS SOUP

My mother created this soup one spring. It's delicious and the secret is to slowly drizzle in the olive oil while the blender is running. Employing this method make this soup creamy and velvety. If you don't, it just tastes like ground up, boiled asparagus which is not nearly as delightful.

asparagus
water
olive oil
salt

Snap the ends off each asparagus. Steam the bottoms you have snapped off separately from the rest of the asparagus spears. Put most of the asparagus spears in the blender with olive oil and salt, reserving a few tips per bowl of soup to use as a garnish. Blend the cooked bottoms in a blender and run them through a food mill to remove the woody bits. Enjoy! It makes a lovely appetizer or a light, refreshing spring dinner.

BHARTA

Bharta is Andrew's favorite Indian dish. You may notice that this version of Bharta has neither hot chili powder nor peas. Andrew does not like chili or peas and this bharta is made to his taste. Bharta was the first Indian dish I set out to learn how to make. I tried recipes from the internet and from numerous cookbooks. I also experimented with different ingredients and ratios in various different kitchens and locals. Finally, after years (literally, I started trying to make this dish when Andrew and I were still dating and didn't create this recipe until nearly our 6th wedding anniversary), Andrew requested that I stop trying to make bharta and just give him a roasted eggplant. And then I wanted to experiment with making vegan marshmallows. So we called up some friends of ours who are Indian and up for experimenting and since they are Indian and up for experimenting, I decided to experiment with making Aloo Saag which is **my** favorite Indian dish. So we made vegan marshmallows. They were a disaster as far as marshmallows are concerned. And they helped me document what I was doing while I tried my first attempt at making saag. After saag was made, there was debate if we should just eat the saag with rice or make roti as well. We decided to make the roti and since roti take some time, and I had a roasted eggplant that I was planning to turn into babaganoush, I decided to make bharta to round out the dishes that we were serving. I knew Andrew wouldn't like it whatsoever I did, so I just did whatever, and the result was "the best bharta I've ever had," according to my husband. Luckily, our friends were in the kitchen with me and busily documenting precisely what I was doing and they captured the recipe found below. I've made the recipe many times since and it's always a winner with my husband, and anyone else who happens to try it.

Heat several tablespoons of oil over medium heat. Then add

1/8 teaspoon cinnamon

1/8 teaspoon cloves

¼ teaspoon cardamom

1 teaspoon coriander

1 teaspoon cumin

When the spices have bloomed, add

1 onion, minced

and cook until tender. Then add

1 large eggplant, roasted

2 tomatoes, chopped

salt to taste

Once the tomatoes are tender, put everything in a blender to puree and then serve with fresh cilantro leaves as a garnish.

BROCCOLI

When I was you I remember my mother serving broccoli as a side dish, lightly steamed with a little fat. This grown up version calls for a squeeze of lemon juice or chili powder to brighten the flavors in addition to olive oil and sea salt.

broccoli, washed
olive oil
sea salt
lemon or chili powder

In a pot with a steamer basket, place the head of broccoli with less than an inch of filtered watered in the bottom of the pan. Cover with a glass lid and place over high heat. If you do not have a glass lid, check after a minute and a half, and every 30 seconds or so after that. You want to remove the broccoli from the heat and also the steamer basket when it turns bright green. The water in the broccoli will continue cooking the tissues, even after you have transferred it to a serving dish which is why so often broccoli is served either tough and hard or yellowed and wilted. Once the broccoli is in the serving dish, sprinkle with sea salt and drizzle with olive oil and a squeeze of lemon. Then use a sharp knife to separate the florets from the stem so that the olive oil and lemon has a chance to drizzle into the cuts you are making. If your broccoli is fresh the trunk of the broccoli tree will be just as delightful as the florets. If your broccoli is somewhat older, before you put it in the pan, use a sharp knife to remove the "bark" from your broccoli tree so that you are cooking only the center of the stem. You will see a distinct change in texture between the center of the broccoli stem and the outer layer if your broccoli is older. If it is new, there will not be a stark difference and you can feel free to enjoy all the parts of the broccoli.

ROASTED BRUSSEL SPROUTS

brussel sprouts
olive oil
salt
red chili powder

Score the bottom of each whole brussel sprout twice to form an X in each stem. Preheat the oven to 400 degrees. Toss the brussel sprouts with olive oil, salt and red chili powder. Place them on a baking sheet in one layer and roast for 20-40 minutes. Periodically shake the pan to brown them evenly.

ROASTED CARROTS

carrots, cut into 1 ½ inch thick slices
olive oil
salt
red chili powder

Preheat the oven to 400 degrees. Toss the carrots with olive oil, salt and red chili powder. Place them on a baking sheet in one layer and roast for approximately 20 minutes.

CELERY STICK RACE CARS

My mother would make these for parties in pre-school and elementary school and they were always a big hit. Adults enjoy them too!

celery stalks, cut in thirds
carrot, sliced into coin shapes
peanut butter
toothpicks

Fill each stalk of celery with peanut butter for the body of the car. Slide toothpicks through the celery so they behave like the axles of the car. Put a carrot wheel on the end of each toothpick and serve.

CALABACITAS

Calabaza is the Spanish word for pumpkin. In northern New Mexico, calabacitas refers to summer squash cooked with onions and or peppers and or corn. According to a New Mexican blog that pops up when you search the internet for calabacitas, "everybody has one and it is the best." Certainly in my family, you can tell who made the calabacitas by what they look like. My mother uses anything from immature pumpkins to patty pan squash, to anything in between. She chops the onion very finely and prefers to use a Spanish onion. She roughly chops the squash and if using frozen corn, puts it in at the same time as the squash. Her favorite is to scrape the corn off the cob making sure to get all the milky part into the dish and that must be done before adding the squash because it takes longer to cook. She covers the corn to help it cook, but does not cover the dish if using frozen corn. My aunt Aurora always used the zucchini variety of summer squash, rarely put corn, and always put chopped green chile. My husband prefers a red onion which he sautes with salt and red chili powder and summer squash varieties that grow in cylindrical shape which he uses a mandoline to slice into slices that are several millimeters thick. He always covers his squash to cook and adds frozen white corn (never corn from the cob) shortly before serving. I like all the varieties of summer squash but prefer it sliced by hand (so that it's less uniform than my husband's but not as chunky as the way my mother makes them) and prefer the slices to be between 3 and 5 millimeters in diameter. I am aware that the point at which I'm am most happy to eat this dish, the thicker pieces are still aldente but the thinner ones have dissolved into mush, some people think it needs more cooking and some people think it is overcooked. Mostly if its corn, squash and onions, or even simply squash and onions with a little salt and chili powder, however it's prepared, I'm happy.

Saute:

1 large onion, minced or sliced

4-8 small summer squash, thinly sliced or roughly chopped

1 package frozen corn, or fresh corn cut off the cob (optional)

2-6 roasted green Anaheim peppers, chopped (optional)

approximately ½ teaspoon red chili powder (optional)

approximately ½ teaspoon salt

After the onions have begun to cook, add the zucchini and then the corn. While the corn and zucchini finish cooking chop the green chili finely. Add the chili and salt to taste.

CALABACITAS COSTA RICAN STYLE

When Jeselle was in Costa Rica, she couldn't get any corn that wasn't canned so she began subsistuting fresh tomatoes for corn and chayote for some of the calabacitas.

Saute:

1 large onion, roughly chopped

4-8 small summer squash, thinly sliced or roughly chopped

fresh chayote, chopped, if available

2-6 fresh tomatoes

approximately ½ teaspoon red chili powder (optional)

approximately ½ teaspoon salt

After the onions have begun to cook, add remaining ingredients. When everything is tender, serve.

SWISS CHARD

This recipe came out of tasting a Lebanese dish called kibbi or kibbeh.

1 large onion

swiss chard, chopped

cooked garbanzo beans

salt

ground sumac

6 tablespoons of lemon juice or 3 grams of vitamin C

olive oil

Cook the onion in olive oil. Add the chard stems. When they are cooked, add the chard leaves. Remove from heat and stir in salt, sumac and lemon to taste. Eat a side dish or use as stuffing for pumpkin kibbeh.

CUCUMBER HORS d'OEUVRES

cucumber, hummus, falafel, tzaziki sauce wrapped in lettuce;

cucumber, potato salad;

cucumber, potato salad, lettuce, sugar snap peas;

cucumber, pesto, roasted bell pepper;

cucumber, veganaise, tomato, avocado;

CELERY ROOT PUREE

Perfect for imparting a subtle celery flavor to breads, soup or mashed potatoes.

Celeraic

Wash and cut all brown surfaces from a celeraic root so that only the white part of the root is remaining. Cut the root into ¼ inch cubes and boil until tender. When the root is tender, mash it in the water you cooked it in.

CROUTONS
stale bread
olive oil
herbs (optional)
salt (optional)

Cut bread into cubes. Toss with olive oil and bake on a cookie tray at 350 until toasted; herbs and salt are optional.

EGGLESS EGG SALAD, AKA TOFU SALAD

In high school, there were occasional days when I didn't take a lunch and really needed to buy something but their only vegetarian option was an egg salad sandwich. At first I would throw away the egg salad and just eat the bread and lettuce after wiping the lettuce off on a napkin, but bread and lettuce isn't satisfying especially when it's been six hours since breakfast and dinner is another six or seven hours away. So I did eat the sandwiches as they were meant to be eaten eventually. I can probably count the number of these sandwiches I actually ate on my fingers. These were not a favorite meal nor something I ate regularly and yet, some twenty years later, for some reason I found myself hungry for one of those sandwiches. I was extremely skeptical that I would like this recipe (though it seemed like the best combination of the recipes I read online) and to my surprise, not only did it remind me of those long ago sandwiches, but I liked it in it's own right. And when my two year old niece was visiting and refusing to eat anything that wasn't bread, she made an exception for this salad.

12 ounces of extra firm tofu, drained
¼ teaspoon turmeric
½ teaspoon salt
½ teaspoon dried dill
¼ teaspoon celery seed
1 ½ teaspoon dijon style mustard
3 tablespoons veganaise
minced onion, to taste (I use a scallion)
minced bell pepper, to taste (I use ¼ of a medium sized green bell pepper)

Take the tofu out of it's water and set it to drain. Combine the herbs and spices in a medium sized mixing bowl with the mustard and veganaise. Mince the onion and bell pepper and add them. Stir thoroughly. Crush handfuls of tofu in your fist to squeeze out all the water before adding the crushed tofu to the mixing bowl. When all the tofu has been added, stir thoroughly. Set the salad in the refrigerator to chill for at least an hour before serving. I like it best the following day.

VEGAN FRITATTA

12 ounces (1 package) extra firm tofu
½ teaspoon turmeric
½ teaspoon chili powder
½ teaspoon salt
herbs
vegetables, chopped
water

put the turmeric and chili powder in a dry ungreased skillet over medium heat to roast the spices and bring out their flavors. In the meantime, put the tofu salt and herbs in a blender with enough water to make a smooth white sauce. Stir the vegetables, tofu and roasted spices together and bake at 350 for about 40 minutes, then reduce to 300 for another 20 minutes or so and serve hot. The first time I made this with 1 red bell pepper, chopped, 1 tablespoon dried basil and 1 teaspoon dried thyme. It was pronounced delicious!

GALETTE de POMMES de TERRE

6 potatoes, thinly sliced
1/3 cup oil
salt to taste (¼ - 1 teaspoon)

Add the salt to the oil. Layer sliced potatoes in a greased 9 inch pie plate. Pour oil evenly over the potatoes. Bake at 400 until potatoes are tender (about an hour). Gently loosen the sides and bottom of the galette with a spatula, then flip onto a serving plate. Cut into wedges to serve.

GARBANZO BEANS WITH ARUGULA

This dish was inspired by a stewed spinach dish in a Spanish cookbook. I'm unwilling to cook greens to a pulp or cook with tomato paste and arugula is easier on my system than spinach, but I really appreciated the combination of paprika, cinnamon and nutmeg with olive oil, garlic, onion and garbanzo beans! The original dish called for minced regular garlic cloves, but by using whole baby cloves, the garlic flavor throughout the dish was softened and muted and the garlic lovers were able to enjoy an intense garlic experience by eating a whole clove.

olive oil
8 whole baby garlic cloves
½ yellow onion, minced
25 ounces canned garbanzo beans, drained
equal amounts salt, paprika, cinnamon and nutmeg to taste (¼ -1 teaspoon)
arugula
fresh or canned tomatoes (optional variation)

Heat the saute pan over medium high heat. Add olive oil, quickly followed by garlic and onion. When the onion is soft, add garbanzo beans and spices. When the spices have infused the olive oil and the garlic cloves are beginning to brown, add arugula. Serve when the arugula is wilted.

GREEN BEANS

green beans
onion, sliced
tomatoes or tomato sauce
olive oil
salt

Gently heat the olive oil and cook the onion over low heat until it is caramelized. When the onion is caramelized, lightly steam the green beans. Add the green beans to the onions and add a few tomatoes or a small amount of tomato sauce. Salt and serve.

KELITE

1 red onion, finely sliced
leaves from immature lambs quarter plants
red bell pepper, optional
salt
chili pequin, optional

Saute the onion. Add the bell pepper, if using. Add the lambs quarter leaves. When wilted, add salt, chili, if using, and serve.

MILLET
1 cup millet
1 tables oil
2 cups water
1 teaspoon salt
Rinse millet and drain completely. Lightly toast millet in oil over moderate heat. Pour in water and salt and bring to a boil. Reduce heat to low and cover the pan with a tight fitting lid. After all the liquid is absorbed, about 20 minutes, let the millet stand for an additional five minutes under the cover of the lid. Fluff and serve while still warm.

MUSHROOM GRAVY
mushrooms
zucchini
tahini
In a food processor, combine 1 pound of crimini mushrooms with 2 medium zucchinis and ¼ cup tahini.

MUSHROOM BURGERS
In my family, a mushroom burger means, sauteed mushrooms on a toasted bun. I am always surprised to see "mushroom burger" on various restaurant menus refer to a decidedly non-vegetarian dish!
mushrooms, sliced
eggplant, sliced (optional)
onions, minced
salt and red chili powder to taste
Saute the onions. Add the mushrooms and eggplant, if using. Season with red chili powder and salt. Serve over toast.

OYSTER MUSHROOMS IN THE HALF SHELL
I first came across something like this at Millennium Restaurant in San Francisco. I was so intrigued that I had to come up with my own version.
oyster mushrooms, sliced
Belgian endive, washed
onions, minced
nori seaweed, crushed
red chili powder to taste
salt to taste
Saute the onions. Add the mushrooms and seasonings. Spoon over individual leaves of Belgian endive and serve chilled.

"OYSTER" MUSHROOMS IN THE HALF SHELL

The last time I wanted to make this recipe, I couldn't find oyster mushrooms or Belgian endive anywhere and we were out of onions, so I improvised and the result was quite tasty!

shitake mushrooms, chopped
Beet tops, washed
green garlic, minced
coconut oil

Saute the garlic in coconut oil. Add the mushrooms. Spoon over individual leaves and serve chilled.

CHILI ONIONS

When I was nursing, I couldn't eat onions and I also had some guests over for brunch and I didn't know if they ate chili, so I made the simple tofu scramble and served it with these onions and steamed asparagus. That was people who wanted the flavor of chili and onions could still enjoy it with the tofu scramble and those who couldn't eat chili or onions could still enjoy brunch!

oil
onions
salt
chili powder

Slice onions thinly. Heat pan. Add a small pool of oil. When the oil is hot, add the onions. When the onions start to change color and texture, add salt and chili powder to taste. Continue cooking until onions are tender.

ROASTED PARSNIPS

I had a low opinion of parsnips until my sister Aja was visiting and made this particularly tasty dish. I felt that parsnips made winter soups too sweet (though I would sometimes use a parsnip in soup anyway) and gave a wonky taste to mashed potatoes. Roasted with olive oil and salt they are deliciously and satisfied my desire for french fries when I was nursing my daughter and couldn't eat white potatoes. They are now a tradition to make on Halloween as a side dish to black beans and rice. You can tell the kids you are serving maggots in dirt and skeleton fingers.

parsnips
olive oil
salt

Cut parsnips into french fry sized pieces. Toss with olive oil and salt and bake at 350 until tender.

FENNEL PEAS

They say necessity is the mother of invention and that is true in cooking as well. When I first went into the health crisis that dramatically changed my eating habits, there was a point when I could not tolerate onions or most oils. My mother made me the following dish and happily I enjoy it enough to make it even when I have other options!

fennel bulb, minced

fennel top, roughly chopped

10 ounces of peas, frozen

almond oil

Mince the bulb of fennel and saute it in almond oil. Add the peas. When the peas are bright green (1-3 minutes), remove from heat and serve with the feathery bits of the fennel bulb that you have chopped up. The heat from the peas and sauteed bulb will nicely wilt the feathery bits as you are eating them, without overcooking them.

PEAS

onion

sunflower oil

peas

herbs

Mince one onion (yellow, white or red). Saute the onion in sunflower oil and add 1 10 ounce package of frozen peas. When the peas are bright green (1-3 minutes), remove from heat and serve. Dried herbs add a nice touch.

ROSEMARY PEAS

1 small onion, finely chopped

1 tablespoons safflower oil

Heat oil and saute onions. When they begin to turn translucent, add

8-16 oz. frozen peas

1 teaspoon dried, ground rosemary, or a few leaves of fresh rosemary, minced

2 teaspoons thyme.

ROASTED RED PEPPERS

peppers

Wash fresh peppers that are firm, not withered. Heat a flat cast iron griddle until a drop of water dances across the surface. This endeavor will be most successful if you can devote your flat skillet solely to roasting vegetables or flat breads. Place the peppers on the griddle until the side on the griddle begins to turn dark brown or black. Turn the peppers before they begin to burn but leave them long enough for the heat to separate the skin from the pepper. Once each side has had a chance to darken, place the peppers in a glass dish with a lid to trap the heat for several minutes to let them sweat. The peppers can then be peeled and used on pizza in pasta or on a salad.

LEMON BASIL MASHED POTATOES
potatoes
oil
basil
lemon juice
salt

Steam 6 baby yukon gold potatoes until tender. When the potatoes are tender mash them with 1-2 tablespoons olive oil. Stir in 4-5 leaves finely chopped fresh basil. Add a squeeze of lemon juice and salt to taste before serving.

PARSLEY POTATOES
potatoes
15- 25 stems parsley
salt
2 tablespoons unsweetened soy milk

Bring to a boil enough water for 6 small red rose potatoes. When the water is boiling, add the potatoes and a teaspoon of salt. When the potatoes are tender mash them with soy milk and parsley.

MOTHER'S BOMBAY STYLE POTATOES
So many cooks are afraid to make Indian food and so many "Indian" recipes call for curry powder to make it easier. Every Indian cook I have ever learned from makes their own "curry" powder by selecting from a tray of spices. This is my favorite combination for Aloo mattar. Enjoy!

1 onion chopped
2 tablespoons sunflower oil
1 teaspoon each of brown mustard seed, red chili powder
½ teaspoon each of salt and turmeric
steamed or baked potatoes, chopped
frozen peas

Place the oil in a large skillet over medium high heat. When the oil is hot add the spices and then saute the onions. When the onions are nearly cooked add the potatoes. Stir constantly to prevent sticking. When the potatoes are a nice golden yellow/brown, add the frozen peas. When the peas are cooked, serve hot.

INDIAN POTATO VARIATION
1 onion chopped
2 tablespoons sunflower oil
1 teaspoon each of brown mustard seeds, coriander seeds, cumin seeds, red chili powder
¼ teaspoon each of ground fenugreek and turmeric
½ teaspoon salt
steamed or baked potatoes, chopped
frozen peas
Place the oil in a large skillet over medium high heat. When the oil is hot add the spices and then saute the onions. When the onions are nearly cooked add the potatoes. Stir constantly to prevent sticking. When the potatoes are a nice golden yellow/brown, add the frozen peas. When the peas are cooked, serve hot.

MASHED POTATOES
boil 1 potato per person, mash with fat, chili powder and salt.
Or
boil 1 potato per person, mash with the water it was cooked in, olive oil and lemon juice
or
boil 1 potato per person, mash with unsweetened soy milk and roasted garlic

GREEN MASHED POTATOES
At one point growing up, my sister refused to eat anything other than potatoes or bread. My mother began making various mashed potato dishes that incorporated vegetables and the whole family happily consumed them.
potatoes
zucchini or broccoli, or both
water
salt
Boil potatoes in water and salt. While the potatoes are cooking, steam the zucchini or broccoli or both. Combine potatoes and steamed vegetables with a potato masher or in a blender. Add liquid from steaming the vegetables if needed to make the potatoes more smooth. Enjoy!

ORANGE MASHED POTATOES
One Easter, my mother baked bread in the shape of an Easter basket. She then made colored "eggs" out of mashed potatoes. The entire dish was a big hit!

mashed potatoes

carrot juice

Make mashed potatoes according to one of the recipes above. Combine mashed potatoes and carrot juice with a potato masher. Enjoy!

PINK MASHED POTATOES

This was the only way I would eat any part of a beet while growing up. Fortunately, my Dad was the only one in the family who liked beets and my mother was the cook. Thus there was never any discussion attempting to get us to eat beets and once in a while, when my mother would make beets for my Dad, I would pour some of the concentrated beet liquid into my potatoes and have pink potatoes for dinner that night. I'm very glad that whenever my mother made beets, she also made mashed potatoes.

potatoes

water

salt

water from steaming beets

Boil potatoes in water and salt. While the potatoes are cooking, steam the beets. Combine potatoes and enough water from steaming the beets using a potato masher or in a blender to make the potatoes smooth. If you love beets, you could mash them with the potatoes and only use enough of the water to make the mixture smooth. If you don't like beets, you can puree them as use them in the carob beet cake. Enjoy!

YELLOW MASHED POTATOES

This dish was created by my mother when my sister refused to eat anything other than bread or potatoes. If the goal is to simply get a yellow in color mashed potato, straight yukon gold potatoes have a lovely yellow hue. However, if your goal is to get your obdurate child to eat something other than bread or potatoes, the yellow crookneck squash hide in these potatoes nicely and will be consumed with gusto!

mashed yukon gold potatoes

yellow crookneck squash

Make mashed potatoes according to one of the recipes above. In the meantime steam the crookneck squash. Combine mashed potatoes and steamed squash with a potato mashed or in a blender. Enjoy!

PEAS

When I went to college, I was having trouble getting enough protein so I called my mother. She let me know that one way to get a complete protein is to combine potatoes with either peas or broccoli. This dish does exactly that!

6 potatoes, washed but not peeled
water
salt
onion, minced
peas
oregano or thyme, optional

Boil the potatoes until tender. In the meantime, saute the onion and the peas, adding the herbs, if using. Mash the potatoes with some of the water they were boiled in and salt to taste. Stir the peas and onions into the potatoes and you will have a complete protein as potatoes and peas, when combined, make a complete protein.

ROASTED ROOT VEGETABLES
carrots
potatoes
olive oil
salt
herbs

Cut tops off carrots and then cut into pieces twice as long as they are wide. Use this size as a guide to cut potatoes to a similar size. The smaller they are cut, the longer the preparation time, but the shorter the cooking time. To achieve even cooking, it is important the vegetables be a uniform size. When everything is, toss with olive oil, sea salt and a fresh herb mix. Bake them at 350 degrees for an hour, or until the potatoes are tender.

ROASTED SPRING POTATOES WITH ROSEMARY AND GARLIC
red skinned potatoes
2-4 carrots
green garlic, finely chopped
the top of 1 carrot, finely chopped
1 sprig fresh dried rosemary, finely chopped
sea salt
olive oil (about 2/3 cup to a cup)

Scrub all the potatoes and carrots and cut into bite sized pieces, but do not peel them. The skins add nice color, not to mention nutrients! Toss the root vegetables in baking pan with the garlic, carrot top, salt, olive oil and rosemary (enough so that each potatoes is coated with a little oil, herbs and salt. Bake at 400 until they begin to turn brown. Approximately every 20 minutes, take them out and stir them. They will take 35 minutes to an hour to roast.

POTATO SALAD
Combine:
potatoes, slightly overcooked to be gluey and then roughly mashed
finely chopped fennel
vegan mayonnaise

QUINOA
I love the serendipity of life. I was unimpressed with any version of quinoa I had ever tasted and thus not overwhelmingly enthusiastic when my doctor recommended I add quinoa to my diet. A few hours later, I noticed quinoa was on sale. So I called my aunt who I had recently connected with after a 17 years to ask if she had any ideas for it's preparation and she shared the recipe below. It is one of her favorite dishes and has become one of mine as well. She advised me not to follow the directions on the box because that will result in a gluey texture and soapy taste. She also opined that quinoa has a delicate nutty flavor but most recipes disguise it by adding tomatoes or something equally overpowering because they don't have the texture right, but with the right texture, you hardly need to do anything to make a delightful dish. I am in agreement with her.
quinoa
water
salt
olive oil
herbs
Boil 4.5 cups of water. When it is a roiling boil, add 2 cups quinoa. Reduce to a simmer, stirring occasionally. When the curly-ques pop, it's done. remove it from heat and gently spoon into a flat dish to cool. If there is water in the pan after the curly-q-ues pop, turn the heat off but leave it in the pan on the burner and it will absorb the extra water. Once it is cooked, add salt, olive oil and herbs. Use a fork to gently fluff it if you like, but do not pat it down or compact it with a spoon, unless you are pressing it into a mold to make a quinoa timbale. Serve warm or cold with or without vegetables. Feeds 4 as a main dish.

QUINOA WITH BELL PEPPERS
quinoa
red bell peppers, finely chopped
basil
olive oil
salt

After cooking the quinoa using the above recipe, toss in bell peppers, salt, basil and olive oil. The heat from the cooling quinoa will lightly cook the bell peppers to perfection!

QUINOA WITH VEGETABLES
quinoa
salt
thyme
olive oil
black olives
zucchini
beet tops from 3 golden beets
baby bok choi
5 small curry leaves
a pinch of turmeric

Boil 4.5 cups of water. When it is a roiling boil, add 2 cups quinoa. Reduce to a simmer, stirring occasionally. When the curly-ques pop, it's done. remove it from heat and gently spoon into a flat dish to cool. If there is water in the pan after the curly-q-ues pop, turn the heat off but leave it in the pan on the burner and it will absorb the extra water. After the quinoa is cooked, toss it with salt, thyme, olive oil and black olives. While the quinoa is cooking, saute the zucchini, beet tops, baby bok choi, curry leaves and turmeric. Spoon the sauteed vegetables over the quinoa. Serves 5.

POTLUCK PERFECT RICE

When I was growing up, my mother would always make this dish for potlucks. There were never any leftovers and always many requests for her recipe.

onion
carrots
rice
celery
mushrooms
turmeric
salt
Saute
1 small onion, thinly sliced
2 finely sliced carrots
1 cup long grain brown rice, rinsed three times in filtered water

When the rice begin to toast, a pleasant aroma will arise and the onions will look somewhat tender. Cover with filtered water until the water level rises 1 inch above the rice. Tightly seal pressure cooker, bring water to a boil, then turn off burner and let the pressure cooker cool on it's own. While the rice is steaming, slice two celery stalks thinly and saute 5-15 button mushrooms with another sliced onion. When the rice is cooked toss the mushrooms, onions, raw celery and ½ teaspoon turmeric into the rice with some salt and fat. The hot rice will cook the celery just the right amount. This dish is now ready to serve immediately or to transport to a pot luck dinner. To reheat after it has been refrigerated, add a little water to the bottom of the pan and heat on low. The rice grains will absorbs the water and return to a tender, rather than a hard consistency.

RICE AND GREENS

Something like this appeared in a book of recipes from around the world dubbed "A Central African Republic Holiday Dish." The author claimed that american spinach made an identical dish to what was served on Central African Republic Holidays thought the author noted that the original recipe called for a local green not available in the Americas. Having never been to CAR, I have no idea how this dish compares with what they serve for holidays, but the recipe below is tasty.

celery seeds
onion
rice
whole peeled tomatoes
water
arugula
salt
Saute
1 teaspoon celery seeds
1 minced onion
2 cups long grain brown rice, rinsed three times in filtered water

When the rice begin to toast, a pleasant aroma will arise and the onions will look somewhat tender. Add one large can of whole peeled tomatoes with basil and 1.5 can's worth of water. Bring to a boil, stir once, then reduce to a simmer and cover with a tightly fitting lid. Let steam for 40 minutes, or until rice is tender. While the rice is steaming, wash two large bunches of arugula and and roughly chop them. When the rice is cooked toss in the chopped arugula and salt to taste (about a teaspoon). The hot rice will cook the arugula just the right amount. The salt will add a finish to the dish without affecting the cooking time of the rice that adding the salt at the beginning would have done. This dish is now ready to transport to a pot luck dinner. If not transporting to a pot luck, let the rice sit on the stove for about 45 minutes, and then enjoy.

SPANISH RICE

This is Spanish rice the way my mother taught me to make it. It is not the dry crusty pink colored rice served is some mexican restaurants. It is most closely approximated by taking left over rice and adding marinara sauce (which I have sometimes done). When compared with "spanish rice" I have been served in restaurants, the latter seems to have more kinship with sawdust than with Spanish rice my mother made for us growing up.

Saute

1 minced onion

2 cups long grain brown rice, rinsed three times in filtered water

When the rice begin to toast, a pleasant aroma will arise and the onions will look somewhat tender. Add

½ teaspoon salt

and enough water to rise one inch above the rice, (about 4 cups.) Bring to a boil, stir once, then reduce to a simmer and cover with a tightly fitting lid. Let steam for 40 minutes, or until rice is tender. While the rice is steaming, make the sauce. The sauce is made by simmering

3 cups tomatoes

oregano to taste

salt to taste

basil, optional

Once the rice is cooked, gently spoon the sauce over it and serve. Chopped olives and celery are optional.

SAGE BREAD

This is a delicate alternative to garlic bread that I especially like to serve in the fall

garlic

fat

sage leaves

bread

Warm ¼ cup oil in a cast iron pan with 4 sage leaves. Spread the liquid fat on a bread of your choice and toast in the oven. If olive oil is is the preferred fat, mince the sage leaves and let the minced sage stand in ¼ cup olive oil for 20 minutes to an hour, before brushing onto the bread and toasting. Heating olive oil before brushing it onto the bread will destroy some of its delicate flavor so it is not recommended!

FAVORITE SANDWICHES

These first require bread and I typically enjoy a sprouted bread or sprouted bun or something equally hearty:

bread, olive oil, lettuce, sprouts, avocado, tomato, mushrooms, cucumber;

bread, veganaise, sprouts;

bread, avocado, sprouts;

bread, avocado, veganaise, sprouts;

bread, veganaise, cucumber;

bread, veganaise, arugula;

bread, veganaise, cucumber, watercress

bread, veganaise, cucumber, avocado, sprouts;

bread, butter, green onions;

bread, butter, green onions, tomato, cucumber, lettuce, sprouts, mushrooms, bell pepper;

bread, veganaise, nature burger, tomato slices, lettuce, sprouts;

bread, pesto, veganaise, nature burger, tomato, lettuce;

bread, olive tapenade, lettuce, tomato, avocado, cucumber, basil, oregano;

chapati, veganaise, tomato slices, lettuce;

GRAIN FREE SANDWICHES

These sandwiches were developed when I couldn't eat any gluten or rice, but still wanted sandwiches. All of the following rely on two sturdy slices of cucumber in place of bread. They work remarkably well as hors d' oeuvres.

cucumber, hummus, falafel, tzaziki sauce wrapped in lettuce;

cucumber, potato salad;

cucumber, potato salad, lettuce, sugar snap peas;

cucumber, pesto, roasted bell pepper;

cucumber, veganaise, tomato, avocado;

SOLANACEA PATTIES

A vegan I know made a recipe like this to take the place of gefilte fish during Passover. We like to eat them whether or not it is Passover.

3 medium potatoes, peeled
2 medium onions, finely chopped
vegetable oil
1 large eggplant
2 tablespoons chopped fresh parsley
sea salt
red chile powder

Boil or steam the potatoes until they are tender, then put them to one side. Preheat the oven to 425°F. Caramelize the onions. Roast the eggplant until the skin starts to shrivel and the flesh is soft. Scoop out the flesh when it has cooked. Turn the oven down to 350°F. Mash the potatoes, add the onion, eggplant, sea salt, and chili powder. Then form the mixture into patties. Put the patties on oiled baking sheets and sprinkle each one with a little oil. Bake them in the oven for 30 minutes until they are golden brown. Serve them hot or cold with salads and horseradish.

SPINACH WITH ONIONS

1 onion
1 bunch spinach
oil

Remove spinach stems from leaves. Mince the onion. Heat oil in pan. Add onion. Chop spinach stems. When the onion is tender add the spinach stems. When the stems begin to cook, add the spinach leaves. Serve with salt or chili wile still bright green.

BRIGHT SQUASH

1 medium red onion, sliced thinly
4 small sunburst squash, sliced
1 bell pepper, diced
1 pound cut corn
salt
red chili powder, optional

Saute the onion and squash. When the squash is half way to being tender, add the bell pepper. When the squash is almost entirely cooked, add the corn, salt and red chili powder.

SUGAR SNAP PEAS

My favorite way to eat sugar snap peas is raw, or possibly with some hummus, but if you are going to cook them, I like this recipe best.

50 mL oil give or take 20 mL
a few cloves of garlic, peeled and thinly sliced
50 mL tamari sauce
mushrooms, optional
sugar snap peas, washed and tips removed
onions, sliced into rings - optional
bell pepper, sliced into thin strips - optional
ginger root, sliced into thin strips - optional
basil, - optional
tahini - optional

Heat a cast iron skillet or other heavy frying pan. Add the oil. When the oil is hot, add the garlic. Stir vigorously so that the garlic doesn't burn. When the garlic is brown, add the tamari sauce and mushrooms, if using. When the mushrooms are cooked, add the onions. When the onions are cooked, add the bell pepper, or any other ingredients if using. When everything is cooked, toss in the sugar snap peas. Turn off the heat but leave in the pan until the sugar snap peas turn bright green. Add a tablespoon or so of tahini, if using, just before serving.

TAPENADE
Puree
green olives
French lentils, cooked
lemon juice to taste
lemon zest from half an organic lemon
olive oil to taste
a few cloves garlic
Serve with crusty bread or crackers.

SAVORY SQUASH TART
winter squash
chili
salt
onion
thyme
soy milk
Combine cooked and pureed squash with a dash of red chili powder and salt, onions that have been sauteed with thyme and enough soy milk to form a soupy consistency. Bake the custard (acorn squash, onions sauteed with thyme, enough soy milk to make it the consistency of unbaked pumpkin pie filling, a dash of red chili powder and sea salt). When the custard is done, I will spoon it into the crust and when it cools, we should have a savory acorn squash tart.

SPINACH TARTINES
onion
fat
spinach
macadamia nut cheese
Saute 1 small onion, thinly sliced, in oil. Add washed, chopped fresh spinach. When the spinach is wilted, remove from heat and serve over 1/8 inch thick slices cheese.

SPINACH TARTINES, RAW VARIATION
onion
sea salt
oil such as olive, walnut, pumpkin seed or sesame
spinach
sun dried tomatoes packed in oil (optional)
macadamia nut cheese
Thinly slice the onion and toss it with washed, chopped fresh spinach, salt and oil. Set aside for 20 minutes or so to let the onion, salt and oil break down the structure of the spinach slightly to give it a wilted appearance. Spoon over "slices" of nut cheese.

STUFFED BELL PEPPERS
2 bell peppers
1 avocado
minced onion
lemon juice
salt

Slice the tops off each pepper and remove seeds. Mash the avocado. Stir in onion and salt. Stuff peppers with avocado mixture, sprinkle with lemon juice (to keep the avocado from turning brown) and garnish with parsley or olives. Serve chilled.

STUFFED ROMA TOMATOES
4 roma tomatoes
1 avocado
minced onion
lemon juice
Salt

Slice each roma tomato in ½ and scoop out the seed. Mash the scooped out seeds with avocado, onion and salt. Stuff tomatoes with avocado mixture, sprinkle with lemon juice (to keep the avocado from turning brown) and garnish with parsley or olives. Serve chilled.

STUFFING
My mom came up with the basis for this recipe when she became a vegetarian. When I became vegan, I discovered that oil, instead of melted butter, is even easier and quite delicious. If you don't add any fat, the stuffing won't brown properly while baking. By the same token, too much fat causes it to brown too quickly.

In a large bowl toss:
1 loaf sprouted barley bread cut into cubes
1 leek washed and sliced into 1/8 inch segments
1 yellow onion chopped
1 handful of chopped celery leaves
1 handful of fresh sage leaves, minced
Sliced mushrooms (optional)
Salt to taste
red chili powder to taste
enough water to plump the bread

When the ingredients are well mixed, transfer to a large baking dish and drizzle with sunflower oil. Stir the stuffing so that the oil is not concentrated in one place and use a knife or toothpick to poke all the non-bread items under the top layer or bread. Anything sticking up above the bread will burn so make sure all the greens are well tucked in. Bake a 350 for 40 minutes or until the top has toasted.

TOFU SCRAMBLE
sesame oil
coriander seeds
cumin seeds
brown mustard seeds
ground turmeric
ground fenugreek
kale
spinach
pea shoots
tofu

Start with a generous circle of oil in the middle of a large cast iron skillet over medium high heat. When the oil is warm, add the seeds. After they toast, add the ground spices. Let the golden and red spices infuse the oil, then add the kale. When the kale is nearly cooked, add the spinach and pea shoots. Lastly add a pound of extra firm tofu, one crushing fistful at a time so it has the consistency of scrambled eggs, going into the pan. Once the tofu absorbs the spices and flavors and heats thoroughly, add salt and serve.

TOFU SCRAMBLE - GREEK STYLE
A description of the way portulaca oleracea is prepared in Greece inspired this delicious recipe!
peanut oil
portulaca oleracea, roughly chopped
three whole peeled tomatoes (canned with basil)
salt
tofu

Start with a generous circle of oil in the middle of a large cast iron skillet and put the stove on medium high heat. Saute the portulaca oleracea. Add a package of extra firm tofu, one crushing fistful at a time so it has the consistency of scrambled eggs, going into the pan. Add the three tomatoes, breaking them up so tomato juice thoroughly soaks the tofu, then add salt to taste.

SIMPLE YUMMY TOFU SCRAMBLE

When Elena was almost one, we invited a few friends and neighbors over on President's Day for a semi spontaneous brunch. We served this tofu scramble with steamed asparagus, chili onions and a drizzle of roasted pumpkin seed oil. Everyone agreed it hit the spot!

oil, enough for form a pool in the center of your pan
turmeric, roughly a teaspoon
brown mustard seeds, roughly 1 ½ teaspoons
fenugreek, roughly ½ teaspoon
tofu, 2 pounds
sea salt, roughly ½ teaspoon

Heat large cast iron skillet over medium high heat. Add oil. When the oil is warm, add ground turmeric, fenugreek, brown mustard seeds and salt. When the spices bloom, add the tofu, one crushing fistful at a time so it has the consistency of scrambled eggs, going into the pan. Alternatively, before heating the pan, you can drain the tofu and add the drained tofu to the hot spice infused oil at this stage, mashing it with a spoon to give it the consistency of scrambled eggs. Serve warm. Store any leftovers in an airtight dish and eat them as you would enjoy egg salad.

TENDER SUMMERY GOODNESS

Every fall, my mother would save pumpkins for thanksgiving, christmas and new year pumpkin pies. The seeds would be carefully scooped out before baking and planted to grow pumpkin for the next year. All summer we would eat the immature pumpkins as a side vegetable, allowing 3-4 grow to maturity to be eaten as pies and planted the following year. The immature pumpkins are so delicious freshly picked from the vine, this recipe is pure tender summery goodness!

onion
baby pumpkins or summer squash
oil

Slice thinly 1 large white or yellow onion. Slice thinly 2-5 immature pumpkins (no larger than a fist) plucked from the vine and washed. Add several tablespoons of an oil of your choice to a large cast iron skillet. Add the onion. When the onion first begins to change color and texture, add the pumpkin. If desired add 1/8 cup of water and cover to steam the pumpkin so that the dish will cook more quickly.

ROASTED VEGETABLE TORTE

Ina Garten made a roasted vegetables torte in one of her cookbooks only her version called for parmesan cheese and possibly eggs. I don't recall exactly what she did, but it inspired me to make the following dish.

onions
zucchini
eggplant
mushrooms, optional
bell peppers, halved
olive oil
salt
red chili powder

Cook zucchini and onions in 2 tablespoons of olive oil in a large saute pan over medium heat until zucchini is tender. Season with salt and NM mild red chili powder. Cook eggplant and onions in the same way. Mushrooms are optional. Brush bell pepper halves or heirloom tomato halves with olive oil, season with salt and chili powder and roast on a baking sheet until soft, but not browned. In a round cake pan, place each vegetable in a single overlapping layer sprinkling Brazil nuts that have been pulsed in the food processor with a clove of garlic between each layer of vegetables. Begin with a layer of eggplant, then zucchini and onions, the roasted vegetables, then zucchini and onions, then eggplant. Cover the top with a layer of parchment paper and a flat disc weighed down by a heavy jar (take precautions to protect fridge from leaks) and chill completely. Drain the liquids to be used in soup later, place on a cake platter and serve.

SPRING VEGETABLES

asparagus or broccoli
olive oil
lemon juice

Lightly steam either asparagus or broccoli. When the vegetables are on the verge of becoming tender, toss them in a cast iron skillet with olive oil until they are tender. Squeeze fresh lemon juice over them to taste. I use approximately half a lemon and a tablespoon of olive oil when I am serving four portions of vegetables.

VERDOLAGAS

According to wikipedia, *portulaca oleracea*, also known as verdolagas, pigweed, purslane, andrakla, glystrida, or Ma Chi Xian contains more omega-3 fatty acids than any other leafy vegetable plant. Simopoulos states that Purslane has 0.01 mg/g of eicosapentaenoic acid, an Omega-3 fatty acid normally found in fish, algae and flax seeds. Purslane also contains vitamin C, vitamin B and carotenoids, as well as magnesium, and iron, two types of betalain alkaloid pigments, the reddish betacyanins (visible in the coloration of the stems) and the yellow betaxanthins (noticeable in the flowers and in the slight yellowish cast of the leaves). These pigment are antioxidants and have antimutagenic properties in laboratory studies. 100 grams of fresh purslane leaves (about 1 cup) contain 300 to 400 mg of alpha-linolenic acid. One cup of cooked leaves contains 90 mg of calcium, 561 mg of potassium, and more than 2,000 IUs of vitamin A. Greeks cook it with tomato, onion, garlic, olive oil and salt. In traditional Chinese medicine, it is used to treat infections or bleeding of the genito-urinary tract as well as dysentery. The fresh herb applied topically relieves sores and insect or snake bites on the skin. Eating purslane can dramatically reduce oral lichen planus. Before my fascinating wikipedia discoveries, all I knew was that in the summer in New Mexico, we would gather verdolagas of medium maturity. The baby plants were so tiny, it was worth letting them grow a few more weeks and the older plants were sometimes more tough and also somewhat bitter. Either my mother or my grandmother would prepare them and serve them with kelite, a pot of beans and homemade flour tortillas. That, to me, was dinner in New Mexico.

onion, minced
portulaca oleracea
oil
salt
chili powder

Saute onion. Add chopped portulaca, chile and salt. Serve when the leaves begin to wilt.

CANDIED YAMS

My brother asked me what temperature to cook yams at and how long they would take. I told him I bake yams at 350 or even 300 and they take at least 40 minutes, but sometimes as long as 2 hours depending in the thickness of the yam and the temperature. Our sister says yams take only 20 minutes, but every time she makes yams the ends are too cooked for me. I discovered she bakes them at 425.

yams or sweet potatoes

Place 1 yam per person in a glass baking dish or on a baking sheet with a rim. Slice each yam with a sharp knife so that steam can escape while baking. Bake at 300 or 350 until each yam is tender, about an hour. If you make sure each yam is approximately the same size, they will all be done at the same time. The lower the temperature, the longer the yams will take to cook, but the more chance the sugars from the yam have to bubble out of the hole you slice in each one to let the steam escape, giving them a candied appearance.

STEAMED YAMS

My mother is always inviting people over, especially around holidays. One year she invited someone she met in the grocery store while shopping for our Thanksgiving dinner. He brought the following dish:

Steam:

3-4 japanese yams, washed

3-4 garnet yams, washed

In a large vegetable steamer in a pot with water up to the bottom of the yams. Cook at a high temperature until the water is hot, then reduce to medium heat. If your pot does not form a tight seal with its lid, you may need to replace the water multiple times during the cooking process. The yams are cooked when their centers are tender. Peel and mash with salt to taste. The skins are a yummy pre-feast treat for kitchen helpers.

5 BEST BREADS

There are some people who say to avoid bread when you are interested in losing weight and other people who say you need bread made from whole grain flour to stabilize your blood sugar level and keep you from crashing. My mother allowed us to eat bread, as long as it was made with whole grain flour, and only one type of flour, and as long as we ate it with vegetables or fat, not with anything sweet like fruit and especially never with jam. If we had a peanut butter sandwich, it was made with bread and peanut butter, no jelly or honey because, "They don't mix!

Whole wheat pastry flour tastes and looks different from Kamut flour or whole grain spelt flour, but the recipes do not need to be modified to accommodate the different flours. None of the recipes in this book will work well with white flour or "all-purpose flour" or "unbleached flour. All of these recipes have been created specifically with whole grain flours in mind and whole wheat pastry flour, whole grain spelt flour and Kamut flour can all be used interchangeably in any of this recipes. Using a non-whole grain flour will lead to a pasty sticky mess. Before discovering that I am quite allergic to wheat, my go to flour was organic whole wheat pastry flour, preferably Bob's Red Mill which is stone ground from a soft white wheat, as opposed to the red wheat many wheat flours are made from. Stone ground flours preserve the oils in the flours, while milling with metal blades tends to denature the oils due to the heat of friction from cutting, as opposed to grinding. Once it was clear that I could not eat wheat without experiencing significant physical pain, I have used primarily spelt flour or Kamut flour in my baking. Spelt flour has sharply shaped grains that tend to cut through gluten so it produces a more crumbly product. To me, it also has a more earthy, nutty flavor than wheat or Kamut flour. Kamut flour is higher in protein and fat than modern wheat flours and produces a softer baked good than spelt or whole wheat. Since spelt and Kamut are both types of wheat, they contain gluten and are not suitable for gluten free diets. In the following recipes, I list the flour I prefer to use for each recipe, but you should feel free to use the whole grain flour you have on hand.

I am still experimenting with gluten free flour mixtures. I have found rice flour to be grainy on its own. Buckwheat and soy flours both have strong after tastes. The after taste of the soy flour is masked if it is less than half the total amount of flour used and I have found a fourth to be an even better quantity. Even a small amount of buckwheat, however, imparts the buckwheat flavor to whatever you are making so Ployes are the only recipe that I enjoy using buckwheat flour in.

ALOO PARATHA

I first had aloo paratha at India Kitchen in Albuquerque. I fell in love. Ajay, cook and owner, always served it with a spicy lemon salt, until many patrons complained it was too hot. Ajay and his wife Rajul are from a northern part of India so their version does not have fresh coriander leaves aka cilantro like many southern versions of aloo paratha. My friend Nalini made aloo paratha for me when I was just going into labor with my first child. She discovered that Kamut flour is very like the chapati flour sold in India so there is no need to make a mixture of white and whole grain flours to attempt to get the correct texture. This recipe is the result of making aloo paratha with Nalini. Hurray! Now we can have aloo paratha whenever we want instead of having to be in New Mexico at a time when India Kitchen is open.

2 cups kamut flour
½ teaspoon salt
oil
water
3-4 potatoes
cumin seeds
brown mustard seed
coriander powder
chili powder
salt
powdered ginger

Boil potatoes. Remove from water and mash. Mix with spices. Mix flour and salt with oil enough water to make a soft dough. Let rest at least 15 minutes. Heat a flat griddle. Break off a piece of dough the size of a golf ball and make a depression in the center. Put potato filling in depression. Cover on all sides with dough and then roll it flat. Brush oil on both sides and cook on the flat griddle. Flip over when bottom is cooked and cook it on the other side.

Serve hot with a sprinkling of lemon juice, chili powder and salt.

BISCUITS LIKE MOM USED TO MAKE

Once in a while, my mom would make biscuits. They were flaky creations that I loved to eat with butter straight from the oven. She never wrote her recipe down and I never watched her enough to figure out what she did so I was delighted to discover the following recipe reproduces the flavor and texture of the biscuits I remember my mother making in my childhood. It was adapted from Babycakes recipe for spelt biscuits which was a recreation of the KFC biscuits that the author remembered from her childhood. After many iterations and slight shifts in ingredients and technique, we came to the following recipe. This has become our go-to recipe when anyone in my family wants to make biscuits.

Preheat oven to 375

In a stand mixer with the paddle attachment, combine

4 cups Kamut flour

2 tablespoons baking powder (yes – I did mean tablespoons, not teaspoons)

1 ½ teaspoons salt

Add

¾ cup oil

1 ½ cup boiling water

When the dry ingredients and wet ingredients are mixed, turn the bowl of the stand mixer upside down onto a pizza stone or stoneware cookie sheet. Press the dough into a roughly rectangle shape that is an even thickness. Score this rectangle with a butter knife or other thick blade so that when the biscuits are baked, you can break off individual biscuits and the sides will still be warm, long after the tops have cooled. Mmm...biscuits.

THYME BISCUITS

One day I wanted biscuits, but didn't have my mother's recipe so I decided to take my scone recipe, omit the sugar and use savory herbs instead of fruit. It worked! and we have been enjoying them ever since. For plain biscuits, simply omit the thyme.

2 cups Kamut flour

2 teaspoons non-aluminum baking powder

½ teaspoon sea salt

4 tablespoons coconut oil

¾-1 cup water

3-5 sprigs of fresh thyme

What to do:

Mix the dry ingredients. Rub in the fat with a pastry cutter or two butter knives. add fresh thyme leaves. Add the water. Spoon onto a cooking sheet and bake for approximately 10 minutes in an oven preheated to 425

BREAD STICKS
2 cups spelt flour
½ teaspoon salt
2 tablespoons coconut oil
½ cup water

Preheat the oven to 425. Mix the dry ingredients. Rub in the fat. Add just enough water to pat into dough with crumbs at the edges. Roll flat. Cut into strips. Twist each strip before putting it on the cookie sheet. Bake at 425 for 8-10 minutes.

BREAD STICK VARIATION
2 cups spelt flour
½ teaspoon salt
½ teaspoon ground ginger
½ teaspoon turmeric
½ teaspoon red chili powder
1 ½ teaspoon brown mustard seeds
2 tablespoons coconut oil
½ cup water

Preheat the oven to 425. Mix the dry ingredients. Rub in the fat. Add just enough water to pat into dough with crumbs at the edges. Roll flat. Cut into strips. Twist each strip before putting it on the cookie sheet. Bake at 425 for 8-10 minutes.

ROSEMARY BREAD STICKS
Did you notice this has half the flour and twice the fat of the two previous recipes? In essence you can make bread sticks with a large variation the the flour to fat ratio. Experiment. Have fun. Enjoy! Relax. Try something new.

1 cup Kamut flour
½ teaspoon salt
½ cup coconut oil
1 tablespoon rosemary leaves (ground if dried, finely chopped if fresh)
5 tablespoons water

Mix flour and salt. Cut fat into the flour until a breadcrumb like mixture is formed. Add the water and rosemary. Roll onto a floured board and chill. Cut into strips and bake on a greased baking sheet for 8-10 minutes in an oven preheated to 400 degrees

HERB STICK VARIATIONS:
Basil, parsley or savory instead of rosemary
Five tablespoons celery root puree instead of water

4 SEED CRACKER RECIPE

Martha Stewart has a 4 seed cracker recipe that calls for black onion seeds. I had never heard of black onion seeds before, nor had Deborah, at Deborah's Natural Gourmet, a store that carries *everything*. The internet clued me in that black onion seeds are sometimes known as black caraway seeds, which Deborah, of course, carries right next to the brown caraway seeds. This recipe produces delightful results, but it is not suitable for people who are sensitive to plants in the lily family, unfortunately. If garlic or raw onion upset your stomach, leave out the black onion seeds and simply make a 3 seed cracker recipe instead.

Mix:

3 cups whole grain spelt flour

2 teaspoons baking powder

1 teaspoon salt

1 tablespoon black onion seeds aka black caraway seeds

1 tablespoon poppy seeds

1 tablespoon black sesame seeds

1 tablespoon unhulled brown sesame seeds

½ teaspoon red chili powder

enough water to make a smooth firm ball of dough (about a cup)

After mixing well, let the dough rest under a clean tea towel while you preheat the oven to 550 or 600 degrees (as hot as it will go). Make sure you have a pizza stone in the lower 1/3 of the oven and that you have removed the top rack. When the oven is preheated, divide the dough into at least 4 pieces. The more pieces you divide it into the easier each piece is to work with but the more time it takes to make all the dough. Roll out each piece as thin as you can and then bake them directly on the pizza stone for about 2 minutes. Longer if you want are really crispy cracker, and less if you want something more tender.

CRACKER VARIATION

Mix:

3 cups whole grain spelt flour

2 teaspoons baking powder

1 teaspoon salt

1 tablespoon black onion seeds aka black caraway seeds

1 tablespoon poppy seeds

1 tablespoon black sesame seeds

1 tablespoon brown mustard seeds

½ teaspoon red chili powder

½ teaspoon cumin

½ teaspoon turmeric

enough water to make a smooth firm ball of dough (about a cup)

After mixing well, let the dough rest under a clean tea towel while you preheat the oven to 550 or 600 degrees (as hot as it will go). Make sure you have a pizza stone in the lower 1/3 of the oven and that you have removed the top rack. When the oven is preheated, divide the dough into at least 4 pieces. The more pieces you divide it into the easier each piece is to work with but the more time it takes to make all the dough. Roll out each piece as thin as you can and then bake them directly on the pizza stone for about 2 minutes. Longer if you want are really crispy cracker, and less if you want something more tender. To serve, put 1/8 teaspoon sal de mer in the center of a salad plate and add a tablespoon of sesame oil and of fresh lemon juice and dip crackers just before eating!

"BUTTERY" CRACKERS

At some point, I was making my cracker recipe from memory and realized I had inadvertently halved the amount of fat my original recipe called for. These are just as delicious as the original version so now, for the most part, they are the version I make when I want a "buttery" cracker.

2 cups Kamut flour
½ teaspoon salt
4 tablespoons coconut oil
5 tablespoons water

Preheat the oven to 425. Mix the dry ingredients. Rub in the fat. Add just enough water to pat into dough with crumbs at the edges. Roll flat. Cut into desired shapes. Bake at 425 for 8-10 minutes.

SUPER "BUTTERY" CRACKERS

I pulled this recipe together for a holiday open house my husband and I hosted just a few months after our wedding. I had rediscovered my body has a rather serious allergic reaction to wheat and wanted there to be some crackers I could eat. I whipped these up using spelt flour and was amazed at how quickly they came together (less then 20 minutes from start to finish) and at the lovely smell that filled the entire apartment building from my baking them. At the party, they were devoured with joyful exclamations and the variety of store bought crackers I had put out remained, for the most part, untouched. Between the marked difference in flavor and substantial difference in price, I have not purchased crackers from the store ever since.

1 cups Kamut flour
½ teaspoon salt
4 tablespoons coconut oil
5 tablespoons water

Mix the dry ingredients. Rub in the fat. Add the water. Roll flat. Cut into strips or fancy cracker shapes before putting it on the cookie sheet. Bake at 425 for 8-10 minutes.

GREEN CHILE CRACKERS

The first time I made these was for my sister as a Christmas present. I had recently acquired some animal cookie cutters the size of cocktail crackers and since I know she goes crazy for all things with chili and had recently been afflicted with her wheat allergy, I wanted to make her some "goldfish" she could eat. I used my basic buttery cracker recipe adding turmeric for color and chili for heat. Of course, I didn't limit myself to goldfish. In addition to fish I made foxes, cows, ducks, horses, dogs, cats, birds, rabbits...

2 cups spelt flour
½ teaspoon salt
¼ teaspoon turmeric
1 teaspoon green chili powder
2 tablespoons coconut oil
½ cup water

Mix the dry ingredients. Rub in the fat. Add the water. Roll flat. Cut into shapes with your favorite cookie cutters and then place them on a cookie sheet. Bake at 425 for 8-10 minutes.

SAVORY CRACKERS

This was the first cracker recipe I ever experimented with. I wanted red and green crackers for the holiday party we were throwing.

2 cups Kamut flour
¼ teaspoon salt
4 tablespoons coconut oil
1 tablespoon dried savory or red chili powder
5 tablespoons water

Preheat the oven to 425. Mix the dry ingredients. Rub in the fat. Add just enough water to pat into dough with crumbs at the edges. Roll flat. Cut into desired shapes. Bake at 425 for 8-10 minutes.

PITA

I have to thank both Bonnie, my aunt with Downs Syndrome and Julia Childs for this recipe. In all of Julia Child's cookbooks, her recipe for Pita bread was the only one that I was willing to try. Unfortunately, it calls for hours and hours of work. Fortunately, I had hours for this experiment. After going through all the steps of massaging the dough, I was getting ready to put them in the oven when Bonnie came into the kitchen and said, "Oh – you're making torties, huh?" At that point I realized that the dough looked very much like my mother's tortilla dough. So the next morning, I made tortilla dough and cooked it the way Julia Childs directed to cook her pita dough. Sure enough, they puffed up beautifully and are every bit as delicious as the ones I spent hours making. And – they only take 10 minutes!

Mix:

3 cups Kamut flour, spelt flour or whole wheat pastry flour

extra flour for rolling out

2 teaspoons baking powder

1 teaspoon salt

with enough filtered water to make a smooth firm ball of dough (about a cup). After mixing well, let the dough rest under a clean tea towel while you preheat the oven to 550 or 600 degrees (as hot as it will go). Make sure you have a pizza stone in the lower 1/3 of the oven and that you have removed the top rack. After the oven is preheated, break off a ping pong sized piece of dough and toss it in a bowl of kamut flour so that it is thoroughly coated, then roll it in a circle shape to a thickness of about a tenth of an inch. (not quite as thin as you can, but almost). If you don't toss it in a bowl of flour before rolling it, after it is rolled, be sure to dust each side with flour. The flour keeps the dough from sticking to your hand as you are putting it in the oven and allows it to puff up instead of sticking to the pizza stone. Place the flat piece of dough directly on the pizza stone and bake it just long enough to puff up (about 2 minutes.) As soon as one is in, begin working on the next pita. You make get up to four on a stone at a time, but usually after the second one it in, it's time to use a long handled metal spatula (like those used for barbequing) to remove the first one. Remove them before they turn hard or change color.

TORTILLAS

The tortilla recipe I use when I want tortillas. More labor intensive than pitas, but handy if you don't have a pizza stone or even an oven. You will notice it has less salt and more baking powder than the recipe my grandmother had me memorize as a child, but does not call for oil. I don't like measuring oil. The added baking powder compensates in fluffiness what removing the oil does for softness. I've never made both recipes side by side and compared to decide exactly how the finished products differ. In my mind they produce an identical outcome: tortillas. Good for serving with beans and spinach and onions in the summer, or eating with potato soup as an alternative to cornbread in the winter. Handy as a sandwich bread the next day...tortillas.

3 cups spelt flour, Kamut flour or whole wheat pastry flour

½ teaspoon salt

2 teaspoon baking powder

1 cup water

Mix the dry ingredients. Add the water. knead the dough while the cast iron flat griddle is heating. Roll the dough out on a floured work space making sure to work it continuously until you put it on the griddle on medium heat. Watch the tortilla puff up on the griddle, flip it when it's puffy and cook it for about the same amount of time on the other side.

REMEMBERED TORTILLA RECIPE

When I was quite young, my grandmother had me memorize this recipe "because no one should need a recipe to make tortillas!"

3 cups flour

1 teaspoon salt

1 teaspoon baking powder

1 cup water

1 tablespoon oil

Mix the dry ingredients and heap them in a bowl, forming a well in the center. Pour the water and oil into the well and knead the dough, but not too much or they will be tough. Pull off balls of dough and roll them out. Cook on a flat cast iron griddle with no fat, hot enough that a drop of water jumps when it comes into contact with the griddle. Watch the tortilla puff up on the griddle, flip it when it's puffy and cook it for about the same amount of time on the other side.

6 ONE DISH WONDERS

All of these dishes can be consumed as a meal in and of themselves, or if you are feeding a larger group, they can be one of several dishes served.

ALOO SAAG

Aloo saag is one of my favorite dishes, and the dish made famous in Andrew's tales of our first date. When I nailed the recipe for Aloo saag, I did a happy dance.

Heat a large sauce pan and add oil. When the oil is hot, add

¾ teapoon of cumin seeds

1 teaspoon of ground turmeric

¼ teaspoon of ground chili powder

When you smell the spices, add a

chopped onion

and let the onion cook in the oil and spices. When the oil is cooked, add

300g baby spinach leaves

300g baby kale leaves

Put in one handful at a time and let it wilt before adding the next handful and stirring. When all the greens are wilted. put everything, including the liquid that may have left the greens in a blender to puree. In the meantime, put

5 tablespoons of fat or oil in a large pan over medium heat. When the oil is hot, add

¾ teaspoons of garahm masala

Then add cooked potatoes or cubed tofu, if using, and when they are coated with the oil and garahm masala, add the spinach mixture.

Thoroughly combine, and then serve.

ARROZ CON PALMITO (VACA MUCA STYLE)

When my husband and I visited my mother in Costa Rica, we took a day to see the Arenal volcano and the La Fortuna waterfall. For dinner that evening, we went to a restaurant called Vaca Muca and I ordered their rice with heart of palm dish. The recipe bellow is my recreation of that meal when I returned to the states. Heart of palm can typically be found in the canned goods section near the canned artichoke hearts.

cooked rice
heart of palm
red bell pepper
oregano
butter
sea salt
onion

Melt 2 tablespoons butter in a skillet. saute heart of palm (sliced), onion and bell pepper. Add rice. eat with Costa Rican style black beans and fried plantains.

BHARTA

Bharta is Andrew's favorite Indian dish. You may notice that this version of Bharta has neither hot chili powder nor peas. Andrew does not like chili or peas and this bharta is made to his taste. Bharta was the first Indian dish I set out to learn how to make. I tried recipes from the internet and from numerous cookbooks. I also experimented with different ingredients and ratios in various different kitchens and locals. Finally, after years (literally, I started trying to make this dish when Andrew and I were still dating and didn't create this recipe until nearly our 6th wedding anniversary), Andrew requested that I stop trying to make bharta and just give him a roasted eggplant. And then I wanted to experiment with making vegan marshmallows. So we called up some friends of ours who are Indian and up for experimenting and since they are Indian and up for experimenting, I decided to experiment with making Aloo Saag which is **my** favorite Indian dish. So we made vegan marshmallows. They were a disaster as far as marshmallows are concerned. And they helped me document what I was doing while I tried my first attempt at making saag. After saag was made, there was debate if we should just eat the saag with rice or make roti as well. We decided to make the roti and since roti take some time, and I had a roasted eggplant that I was planning to turn into babaganoush, I decided to make bharta to round out the dishes that we were serving. I knew Andrew wouldn't like it whatsoever I did, so I just did whatever, and the result was "the best bharta I've ever had," according to my husband. Luckily, our friends were in the kitchen with me and busily documenting precisely what I was doing and they captured the recipe found below. I've made the recipe many times since and it's always a winner with my husband, and anyone else who happens to try it.

Heat several tablespoons of oil over medium heat. Then add

1/8 teaspoon cinnamon
1/8 teaspoon cloves
¼ teaspoon cardamom
1 teaspoon coriander
1 teaspoon cumin

When the spices have bloomed, add

1 onion, minced

and cook until tender. Then add

1 large eggplant, roasted
2 tomatoes, chopped
salt to taste

Once the tomatoes are tender, put everything in a blender to puree and then serve with fresh cilantro leaves as a garnish.

BREAKFAST BURRITO
potatoes fried with onion
or left over mashed potatoes
ranchos style salsa
tortillas (1 per burrito)

Warm the tortilla, or don't – then put it on a dinner place. Spread potatoes down the middle about an 1-2 inches wide, leaving 2 inches at at least one end. Top with ranchos style salsa, or the salsa or chili of your choice. Fold the end(s) where you have left two inches over the potatoes, then fold one of the side over and roll it up. For your second serving, adjust the amount of filling as desired. Too much filling and it will fall out all over the plate. Too little filling and you will be eating mostly tortilla.

EL PATIO BURRITO

I whipped out the red chile sauce I made last night when I was hungry for my grandmother's boiled potatoes in chile, heated up some beans (with onion, ginger, and soy sauce, of course), put the beans in the tortilla rolled it with the ends on the bottom (just like they do at El Patio), covered it with the chile, sliced some pepper jack thinly on top and popped it in the oven on broil until the cheese melted - mmm, mmmm... It was even better than El Patio's and it was all organic. and I didn't have to worry about forgetting to request a whole wheat tortilla, and I wasn't tempted by the nasty white flour sopapilla that I always think will taste good but that in fact never tastes good and almost always makes my stomach ache!

86

EGGLES EGG SALAD, AKA TOFU SALAD

When my two year old niece was visiting and refusing to eat anything that wasn't bread, she made an exception for this salad.

12 ounces of extra firm tofu, drained

¼ teaspoon turmeric

½ teaspoon salt

½ teaspoon dried dill

¼ teaspoon celery seed

1 ½ teaspoon dijon style mustard

3 tablespoons veganaise

minced onion, to taste (I use a scallion)

minced bell pepper, to taste (I use ¼ of a medium sized green bell pepper)

Take the tofu out of it's water and set it to drain. Combine the herbs and spices in a medium sized mixing bowl with the mustard and veganaise. Mince the onion and bell pepper and add them. Stir thoroughly. Crush handfuls of tofu in your fist to squeeze out all the water before adding the crushed tofu to the mixing bowl. When all the tofu has been added, stir thoroughly. Set the salad in the refrigerator to chill for at least an hour before serving. I like it best the following day.

ENCHILADAS

Make a red chili sauce. Put red chili powder and flour in a dry skillet. Turn the heat on high and stir constantly. When the smell of the chili and toasting flour fills the kitchen but before it begins to darken, transfer to a sauce pan with 2 tablespoons oil and add water. Cook the sauce over medium heat (warm enough to form little bubbles, cool enough not to be a roiling boil) stirring constantly (to prevent formation of lumps) until the sauce begins to thicken. If the sauce is beginning to thicken and there are still some lumps, you can pour it into a blender and buzz it a few times to get the lumps out. Add salt to taste before pouring the sauce over anything. The ratio of chili powder to flour will affect the heat of the finished sauce. To start out I use 4 tablespoons red chili, 4 tablespoons flour, 4 cups water, 2 tablespoons sunflower oil, 1 teaspoon salt. If the sauce is too hot, the next time I will use 2 tablespoons chili and 6 tablespoons flour. If it is not hot enough I might use 6 tablespoons red chili powder and 2 tablespoons flour. The gluten in the flour is what causes the sauce to thicken.

While cooking the sauce, toast a dozen corn tortillas in the oven until they are crispy. Chop an onion finely. When the red chili is ready, put a corn tortilla in the red chili sauce then grab another tortilla and use it to catch any chili that drips from the first tortilla as you transfer it from the sauce to the baking dish you are using to make the enchilada. Putting the tortillas in the sauce with cause them to soften. This is why you want them crisp initially. If they curl while toasting, no problem. Once you put them in the sauce they will unfurl. Layer the tortillas in the bottom of the baking dish, putting a layer of chopped raw onion just under the top layer of tortillas. Bake in the oven at 350 for 20-30 minutes.

FRITO PIE

Growing up in New Mexico, I remember when my mother wasn't around, my aunt buying us frito pies when we went to the mall in Santa Fe. I don't even know if they make fritos any more, but I do know my mother didn't approve of them based on their non-organic origins and hydrogenated oil. Of course, now that basically all corn is genetically modified, buying fritos is out of the question. However, the concept of frito pie still works.

a hand full of corn chips

a serving of beans

salsa

In your bowl, place a handful of corn chips. Cover the corn chips with a ladelful (or two) of hot juicy beans. Cover the beans with salsa and enjoy.

GALLO PINTO

In Costa Rica there is a saying that translastes as "without beans and rice, it isn't food." In other words, unless what you are serving includes both beans and rice, it's not a meal, it is merely a snack. Gallo Pinto is frequently eaten for breakfasts and the basic recipe is to take cooked rice and cooked black beans and heat them in a frying pan with some oil until the dish is warm and the rice has absorbed the bean juice taking on a speckled hue. This dish can have onion, carrots, heart of palm, bell pepper or any other vegetable that you might cook with rice. If you did not start out with black beans prepared in the Costa Rican style, add oregano. Before eating, squeeze lime juice and sprinkle fresh chopped cilantro over the top.

GARBANZO BEANS, SPANISH STYLE

This dish was inspired by a stewed spinach dish in a Spanish cookbook. I'm unwilling to cook greens to a pulp or cook with tomato paste and arugula is easier on my system than spinach, but I really appreciated the combination of paprika, cinnamon and nutmeg with olive oil, garlic, onion and garbanzo beans! The original dish called for minced regular garlic cloves, but by using whole baby cloves, the garlic flavor throughout the dish was softened and muted and the garlic lovers were able to enjoy an intense garlic experience by eating a whole clove.

olive oil

8 whole baby garlic cloves

½ yellow onion, minced

25 ounces canned garbanzo beans, drained

equal amounts salt, paprika, cinnamon and nutmeg to taste (¼ -1 teaspoon)

arugula

fresh or canned tomatoes (optional variation)

Heat the saute pan over medium high heat. Add olive oil, quickly followed by garlic and onion. When the onion is soft, add garbanzo beans and spices. When the spices have infused the olive oil and the garlic cloves are beginning to brown, add arugula. Serve when the arugula is wilted.

GREEN BEANS

In America, green beans are typically a side dish and appear most often as a goupy caserole at Thanksgiving. These green beans are so delicious and filling they easily can become the entire meal.

green beans

onion, sliced

tomatoes or tomato sauce

olive oil

salt

Gently heat the olive oil and cook the onion over low heat until it is caramelized. When the onion is caramelized, lightly steam the green beans. Add the green beans to the onions and add a few tomatoes or a small amount of tomato sauce. Salt and serve.

KIBBI

I had never heard of kibbi, also sometimes written kibbeh, until Samira, who is Lebanese offered me some vegetarian kibbi at the Lexington Farmer's Market. I was in love, and immediately spurned to do research. Traditionally it's made with meat, but during fast days, it's made with bulgar wheat and pumpkin and the name translates to English as "lying kibbi" because they look like the meat dish, but are vegetarian. I found a video on the internet attributed to Taste of Beirut, and armed with the video and the sample from Samira, and my own natural laziness, I decided to make a kibbiesque dish. It was a ringing success.

1 onion, weighing about 300 grams
1200 grams cooked pumpkin
1 teaspoon salt
½ teaspoon chili powder
500 grams of stale bread
olive oil
2 onions, weighing about 300 grams each
400 – 600 grams swiss chard, chopped – stems separated out
1 teaspoon salt
2 tablespoons ground sumac
6 tablespoons lemon juice or 3 grams of vitamin C (asorbic acid)
cooked garbanzo beans

Put an onion in the food processor until it is pulp. Add pumpkin, salt and chili powder. Turn the bread into breadcrumbs. (I used the food processor grater blade to do this) and combine the breadcrumbs and the pumpkin mixture. Preheat the oven to 375. Mince the other 2 onions. Cook them in olive oil. When they are tender, add the chard stems. When the stems are cooked, add the chopped chard leaves. When they are wilted, removed it from heat and add salt, sumac and lemon or asorbic acid and garbanzo beans. Generously oil two 8x8 baking dishes. Put ¼ of the pumpkin mixture into the bottom of each dish. Spoon a layer of the chard mixture into each dish (you may have chard left over – that's okay). Cover with the remaining pumpkin mixture. Pour oil over the top and then bake at 375 for about an hour.

MUSHROOM BURGERS

In my family, a mushroom burger means, sauteed mushrooms on a toasted bun. I am always surprised to see "mushroom burger" on various restaurant menus refer to a decidedly non-vegetarian dish!

mushrooms, sliced
eggplant, sliced (optional)
onions, minced
salt and red chili powder to taste

Saute the onions. Add the mushrooms and eggplant, if using. Season with red chili powder and salt. Serve over toast.

EGGPLANT MANICOTTI

Andrew invented this recipe one night when he was hungry for a vegan, gluten free casserole that reminded him of eggplant parmesan, and it has become a family favorite. If it weren't so labor intensive, I would make it weekly when eggplant is in season. As it is, we eat it as often as Andrew is excited about making it. This dish works best if you use a mandolin to slice the eggplant. The eggplant must be sliced thinly, less than 1/8 inch and it must be rolled rather than laid flat. For some reason when the eggplant is laid flat, the texture is unappealing.

Eggplant, thinly sliced
White Sauce made from:
tofu
dried basil
olive oil
salt
water
Andrew's Marinara sauce, or your favorite marinara.

Slice the eggplant thinly with a mandolin. Combine tofu, basil, olive oil, salt, and water, if needed in a blender to form a white sauce. Make marinara sauce. Roll each slice of eggplant into a tube so it resembles a manicotti noodle. This won't work if your eggplant is too thick! Using a mandolin will get the eggplant 1/8" thin, or thinner! If you don't have a mandolin, be prepared to be handy with your knife! Stuff each "noodle" with the tofu mixture and place in a baking dish. When the baking dish is filled, cover with marinara sauce and bake at 350 for half an hour or at 300 for an hour and a half.

DUSHENKA'S VERSION OF ANDREW'S LASAGNA

This is what the original lasagna recipe found below has evolved into over the years of making it.

arugula
2 large onions
muir glen crushed tomatoes with basil
sun dried tomatoes packed in olive oil
1 pound tofu
salt
oregano
lasagna noodles
oil

Put a large stock pot of water on to boil. Mince one onion to make Andrew's marinara sauce with the crushed tomatoes, thyme, oregano and salt. Slice the second onion and put that in a medium sized stock pot to caramelize. Wash the arugula. When the water for the noodles is boiling, add salt and then the noodles, moving them with a fork so they are not touching one another. Check on them periodically to make sure they don't touch as they are cooking. Put a thin layer of marinara sauce in the bottom of the lasagna pan. This prevents the noodles from sticking on the bottom of the pan. When the onions are caramelized, add the arugula and stir until wilted. When the noodles are cooked, drain them and rinse them in cold filtered water to arrest the cooking process. As you are rinsing them in water, quickly place the first layer of noodles to the bottom of the lasagna pan. Take the remaining noodles and place them flat on cutting boards so that they do not stick together while you are assembling the rest of the lasagna. If you haven't already done so, Put one pound of tofu in the blender with olive oil from a jar of sun dried tomatoes. This will not be enough liquid to make a creamy sauce, so put 2-3 tablespoons water in the sun dried tomato jar and shake it well to get more particles of oil into the lasagna. Add salt to taste. Pour tofu onto the noodles in the lasagna pan. Cover with noodles. Cover with arugula and onions, being careful that none of the juice from the cooked arugula goes into the pan. Add sun dried tomatoes. Cover with noodles. Pour marinara sauce over the top. Bake at 300 for about an hour and a half...mmm...lasagna.

RAW LASAGNA
Use an assortment of vegetables listed below:
squash
carrots
eggplants
bell pepper
cashew cheese
raw marinara sauce or tomato "creme" sauce

To make lasagna, thinly slice vegetables and layer with the cashew cheese, best pesto evar and tomato "creme" sauce or a raw marinara sauce made by putting fresh tomatoes in a blender with dried herbs and salt.

HERBED PASTA
Cook four servings of your favorite pasta. After draining it, add enough olive oil so that it doesn't stick. Toss it with one of the following herb combinations:

1 tablespoon dried basil, 1 ½ teaspoon dried oregano, ½ teaspoon salt;

1 ½ teaspoon dried basil, 1 ½ teaspoon dried oregano, ½ teaspoon salt;

2 tablespoons each of Mexican oregano, red chili seeds or flakes, ½ teaspoon salt;

2 tablespoons fresh thyme, chopped and 1 tablespoon dried basil, 1 teaspoon salt;

4 sprigs fresh basil chopped and 1 tablespoon dried parsley;

1 tablespoon each red chili flakes and ground dried rosemary, 1 teaspoon salt

PARTY PASTA
Cook bow tie, spiral, penne or trumpet pasta normally. As soon as it has been drained toss in olive oil, raw snow peas and cherry tomatoes, halved, chopped green onion, 12-20 leaves fresh basil, chopped, 1 tablespoon dried oregano, 1 teaspoon salt. The heat from the pasta will cook the peas and tomatoes to perfection. Serve immediately, garnishing with a few whole leaves of fresh basil.

PASTA WITH VEGETABLES
While the pasta is cooking, saute the vegetables. I begin with the most firm to the most delicate and add one vegetable to the saute at a time, letting each vegetable begin to cook before adding the next. Favorite combinations are:

artichoke hearts, lemon juice, parsley;

carrots, broccoli, yellow squash, asparagus, bell pepper, tomatoes, snow peas, butter;

carrots, broccoli, yellow squash, mushrooms, asparagus, bell pepper, tomatoes, snow peas, butter;

eggplant, tomato, basil;

eggplant, tomato, basil, thyme, rosemary;

fresh tomato, fresh basil;

fresh tomato, fresh basil, green onions

Pasta with Vegetables continued...

fresh tomato, red chili flakes, salt;

fresh tomato, red chili flakes, garlic

fresh tomatoes, green garlic, salt;

garlic, tomato;

garlic, olives, tomato, red chili flakes

leeks, red, white, green onions, parsley, salt;

onions, Japanese eggplant, bell pepper, mushrooms, dried basil, parsley, chili, salt, fresh tomato;

onions, Japanese eggplant, bell pepper, mushrooms, dried basil, parsley, chili, salt, olives, fresh tomato;

white onion, minced, crimini mushrooms, thinly sliced, red chili flakes, ground dried rosemary, salt;

onions, asparagus, tomatoes, snow peas, fresh basil, dried oregano, butter, salt;

onion, butternut squash, sage, salt;

onion, butternut squash, celery, chili, ginger, sage, salt;

onion, butternut squash, fresh sage leaves sauteed in butter;

onion, green bell peppers;

onion, green bell peppers, basil, salt;

onion, bell peppers, mushrooms, basil, salt;

onions, squash blossoms, salt;

onions, eggplant, tomato, basil, (rosemary) (thyme)

onion, spinach, red chili flakes, salt;

onion, spinach, tomato, red chili flakes, salt;

red onion, tomatoes,arugula, salt;

oyster mushroom, green onions, butter;

All of these dishes are made with pasta and vegetables and opposed to pasta and sauce.

SUMMER PASTA
fettuccine pasta
fresh broccoli
tomatoes
snow peas
bell peppers
onion

While the pasta is cooking, lightly saute the vegetables beginning with the onion, then the peppers then the broccoli. When the broccoli is tender and bright green (before it turns yellow from overcooking) remove the vegetables from the heat. Toss over cooked pasta with olive oil, salt, red chili, and the uncooked snow peas and tomatoes. The heat from the pasta will cook the peas and tomatoes to perfection. Serve immediately.

PAD THAI STYLE ZUCCHINI "PASTA"
zucchini
garlic
soy sauce
lemon juice
agave nectar
chili
green onion
peanuts
lime juice

Slice summer squash through mandolin on thinnest setting (about 2 medium squash per person). Feed squash slices through pasta maker (or slice by hand into fettuccine sized strips). Put oil in pan on high heat. And 2 cloves of minced garlic and let brown. Then add soy sauce, lemon juice, agave nectar and chili. Stir together and add squash. When squash is "aldente" (some pieces are thoroughly cooked and some are closer to raw than to cooked) remove from heat and add green onion, roughly chopped peanuts and a squeeze of lime juice.

THAI ORCHID INSPIRED "PASTA"
When Andrew and I were dating, we would sometimes eat lunch at a restaurant in Albuquerque called Thai Orchid. I was hungry for something like what we used to order for lunch, but living on the east coast so I made the following.

1 clove garlic, sliced
½ thumb length of ginger root, julienne
1 stem of fresh basil, roughly chopped
green bell pepper, sliced
6 mushrooms, sliced
12 ounces mung bean sprouts
1 teaspoon sesame oil
2 tablespoons tamari sauce
2 tablespoons agave nectar
1 teaspoon rice vinegar
½ teaspoon himalayan sea salt

Saute garlic, ginger and basil stems. Combine sesame oil, tamari sauce, agave nectar, vinegar and salt in a small bowl and set aside. When the garlic, ginger and basil stems are tender, add all vegetables, except the mung bean sprouts. When the vegetables are cooked, add the mung bean sprouts and stir over low heat until the mung bean sprouts have the consistency of aldente pasta (less than a minute). Serve with roasted salted cashews.

MOTHER'S RECIPE FOR POLENTA

water
coarsely ground cornmeal
olive oil
salt

Put as much water in a pot as you would like polenta. Bring this to a boil. Add salt once it is boiling. When the salted water is boiling, with one hand begin whisking the water in a circular motion. With the other hand begin pouring the polenta grains into the boiling water that is being whisked a few grains at a time. When the pot seems like it has a polenta mixture, rather than a few grains of polenta in a large pot of water, stop adding polenta, but continue whisking. Whisk constantly to prevent lumps from forming as the polenta cooks. When it thickens, the polenta is finished cooking. Pour olive oil into it while continuing to whisk. When the olive oil is whisked in, serve it immediately with tomato sauce, onions and greens and olive oil, or pour it into a casserole dish to use in a casserole

POLENTA CASEROLE

I did not consider myself a fan of polenta until I tasted a casserole like this at a potluck once. Then, of course, I had my mother's polenta, which wasn't something she ever made when we were growing up, and now, between the two recipes, coarse organic cornmeal has become something that I like to always have on hand. That way there is always polenta for dinner, if nothing else.

polenta
beans
tomato sauce

Make polenta and pour it into a casserole dish. Cover the polenta with a layer of beans. I prefer pinto beans, but black beans also work. Cover the beans with a layer of marinara sauce. Bake at 300 for about an hour or 350 or even 375 until everything is warm. Baking it a lower temperature will make sure it's not soupy. But then, sometimes I like it soupy.

PAD THAI (Tofu, no egg)

This looks like a complicated recipe, but it's actually quite simple once you make it.

SAUCE

1 tablespoon tamarind concentrate

2/3 cup boiling water

3 tablespoons tamari sauce

3 tablespoons agave nectar

2 tablespoons oil

1 tablespoon rice vinegar

¾ teaspoon chili powder

Dissolve tamarind concentrate in boiling water. Add remaining sauce ingredients, then set aside.

NOODLES

8 ounces flat rice noodles

4 quarts water

Bring the water to a boil then remove from heat and add noodles. Let stand, stirring occasionally about 10 minutes. Drain noodles and set aside.

ASSEMBLY

Saute over medium heat, until lightly browned:

2-3 cloves minced garlic

1 shallot, minced

Stir in

tofu, chopped

Add

rice noodles, drained

sauce

increase heat to high and cook, tossing constantly until the noodles are well covered, about a minute.

Add

3 cups mung bean sprouts

3 scallions, chopped

¼ cup peanuts, chopped

Continue tossing constantly until noodles are tender, 2-3 minutes. If not tender after 3 minutes, add 2 tablespoons water to the skillet and continue to cook until tender.

Transfer the noodles to a serving platter and add

2 cups mung bean sprouts

2 scallions, chopped

¼ cup peanuts, chopped

½ teaspoon chili flakes

Gently stir together and serve immediately with lime wedges to be squeezed over each individual serving.

SESAME NOODLES
cooked noodles
2 tablespoons tamari sauce
1 teaspoon sesame oil
2 tablespoons sesame seeds
lemon juice
In a dry skillet heat sesame seeds over medium heat until they smell toasted. Add the sesame oil, tamari sauce, cooked noodles and remove from heat. Just before eating, add a squeeze of fresh lemon juice to each serving and additional salt if desired.

SUN-DRIED TOMATO SUNFLOWER SEED PATE
This recipe came from reading a raw food dish called "mock salmon." Their recipe sounded gross, but it did inspire this dish which inspired my raw tomato cream sauce and also my best pesto ever variation! Hurrah for inspiration!
1 small onion, thinly sliced
½ cup tamari sauce
2 thin cloves garlic or 1 medium clove, peeled
2 cups sunflower seeds
juice from 1 lemon
¾ cup water
1 jar sun dried tomatoes packed in olive oil
Marinate the onions in the tamari for several hours. Put garlic in the food processor and pulse until minced. Add sunflower seeds and pulse until a fine crumb is formed. Add lemon juice and as much water as needed to get the consistency of pate. Remove onions from tamari and set tamari aside for some other recipe that calls for tamari sauce. Add onions and sun dried tomatoes and pulse until a paste is achieved. Serve into a cheesecloth lined mold or a dipping bowl and remove from mold to slice thinly as a pate and sprinkle with herbs and spices such as dill, cumin or fenugreek, or serve with vegetable crudites as a yummy dip.

INDIAN STYLE POTATOES
So many cooks are afraid to make Indian food and so many "Indian" recipes call for curry powder to make it easier. Every Indian cook I have ever learned from makes their own "curry" powder by selecting from a tray of spices. This is my favorite combination for Aloo mattar. Enjoy!
1 onion chopped
2 tablespoons sunflower oil
1 teaspoon each of brown mustard seed, red chili powder
½ teaspoon each of salt and turmeric
steamed or baked potatoes, chopped

frozen peas

Place the oil in a large skillet over medium high heat. When the oil is hot add the spices and then saute the onions. When the onions are nearly cooked add the potatoes. Stir constantly to prevent sticking. When the potatoes are a nice golden yellow/brown, add the frozen peas. When the peas are cooked, serve hot.

QUINOA

I love the serendipity of life. I was unimpressed with any version of quinoa I had ever tasted and thus not overwhelmingly enthusiastic when my doctor recommended I add quinoa to my diet. A few hours later, I noticed quinoa was on sale. So I called my aunt who I had recently connected with after a 17 years to ask if she had any ideas for it's preparation and she shared the recipe below. It is one of her favorite dishes and has become one of mine as well. She advised me not to follow the directions on the box because that will result in a gluey texture and soapy taste. She also opined that quinoa has a delicate nutty flavor but most recipes disguise it by adding tomatoes or something equally overpowering because they don't have the texture right, but with the right texture, you hardly need to do anything to make a delightful dish. I am in agreement with her.

quinoa
water
salt
olive oil
herbs

Boil 4.5 cups of water. When it is a roiling boil, add 2 cups quinoa. Reduce to a simmer, stirring occasionally. When the curly-ques pop, it's done. remove it from heat and gently spoon into a flat dish to cool. If there is water in the pan after the curly-q-ues pop, turn the heat off but leave it in the pan on the burner and it will absorb the extra water. Once it is cooked, add salt, olive oil and herbs. Use a fork to gently fluff it if you like, but do not pat it down or compact it with a spoon, unless you are pressing it into a mold to make a quinoa timbale. Serve warm or cold with or without vegetables. Feeds 4 as a main dish.

QUINOA WITH BELL PEPPERS

quinoa
red bell peppers, finely chopped
basil
olive oil
salt

After cooking the quinoa using the above recipe, toss in bell peppers, salt, basil and olive oil. The heat from the cooling quinoa will lightly cook the bell peppers to perfection!

QUINOA WITH VEGETABLES
quinoa
salt
thyme
olive oil
black olives
zucchini
beet tops from 3 golden beets
baby bok choi
5 small curry leaves
a pinch of turmeric

Boil 4.5 cups of water. When it is a roiling boil, add 2 cups quinoa. Reduce to a simmer, stirring occasionally. When the curly-ques pop, it's done. remove it from heat and gently spoon into a flat dish to cool. If there is water in the pan after the curly-q-ues pop, turn the heat off but leave it in the pan on the burner and it will absorb the extra water. After the quinoa is cooked, toss it with salt, thyme, olive oil and black olives. While the quinoa is cooking, saute the zucchini, beet tops, baby bok choi, curry leaves and turmeric. Spoon the sauteed vegetables over the quinoa. Serves 5.

POTLUCK PERFECT RICE

When I was growing up, my mother would always make this dish for potlucks. There were never any leftovers and always many requests for her recipe.

onion
carrots
rice
celery
mushrooms
turmeric
salt
Saute
1 small onion, thinly sliced
2 finely sliced carrots
1 cup long grain brown rice, rinsed three times in filtered water

When the rice begin to toast, a pleasant aroma will arise and the onions will look somewhat tender. Cover with filtered water until the water level rises 1 inch above the rice. Tightly seal pressure cooker, bring water to a boil, then turn off burner and let the pressure cooker cool on it's own. While the rice is steaming, slice two celery stalks thinly and saute 5-15 button mushrooms with another sliced onion. When the rice is cooked toss the mushrooms, onions, raw celery and ½ teaspoon turmeric into the rice with some salt and fat. The hot rice will cook the celery just the right amount. This dish is now ready to serve immediately or to transport to a pot luck dinner. To reheat after it has been refrigerated, add a little water to the bottom of the pan and heat on low. The rice grains will absorbs the water and return to a tender, rather than a hard consistency.

RICE AND GREENS

Something like this appeared in a book of recipes from around the world dubbed "A Central African Republic Holiday Dish." The author claimed that american spinach made an identical dish to what was served on Central African Republic Holidays thought the author noted that the original recipe called for a local green not available in the Americas. Having never been to CAR, I have no idea how this dish compares with what they serve for holidays, but the recipe below is tasty.

celery seeds
onion
rice
whole peeled tomatoes
water
arugula
salt

Saute

1 teaspoon celery seeds

1 minced onion

2 cups long grain brown rice, rinsed three times in filtered water

When the rice begin to toast, a pleasant aroma will arise and the onions will look somewhat tender. Add one large can of whole peeled tomatoes with basil and 1.5 can's worth of water. Bring to a boil, stir once, then reduce to a simmer and cover with a tightly fitting lid. Let steam for 40 minutes, or until rice is tender. While the rice is steaming, wash two large bunches of arugula and and roughly chop them. When the rice is cooked toss in the chopped arugula and salt to taste (about a teaspoon). The hot rice will cook the arugula just the right amount. The salt will add a finish to the dish without affecting the cooking time of the rice that adding the salt at the beginning would have done. This dish is now ready to transport to a pot luck dinner. If not transporting to a pot luck, let the rice sit on the stove for about 45 minutes, and then enjoy.

SPANISH RICE

This is Spanish rice the way my mother taught me to make it. It is not the dry crusty pink colored rice served is some mexican restaurants. It is most closely approximated by taking left over rice and adding marinara sauce (which I have sometimes done). When compared with "spanish rice" I have been served in restaurants, the latter seems to have more kinship with sawdust than with Spanish rice my mother made for us growing up.

Saute

1 minced onion

2 cups long grain brown rice, rinsed three times in filtered water

When the rice begin to toast, a pleasant aroma will arise and the onions will look somewhat tender. Add

½ teaspoon salt

and enough water to rise one inch above the rice, (about 4 cups.) Bring to a boil, stir once, then reduce to a simmer and cover with a tightly fitting lid. Let steam for 40 minutes, or until rice is tender. While the rice is steaming, make the sauce. The sauce is made by simmering

3 cups tomatoes

oregano to taste

salt to taste

basil, optional

Once the rice is cooked, gently spoon the sauce over it and serve. Chopped olives and celery are optional.

SOLANACEA PATTIES

A vegan I know made a recipe like this to take the place of gefilte fish during Passover. We like to eat them whether or not it is Passover.

3 medium potatoes, peeled
2 medium onions, finely chopped
vegetable oil
1 large eggplant
2 tablespoons chopped fresh parsley
sea salt
red chile powder

Boil or steam the potatoes until they are tender, then put them to one side. Preheat the oven to 425°F. Caramelize the onions. Roast the eggplant until the skin starts to shrivel and the flesh is soft. Scoop out the flesh when it has cooked. Turn the oven down to 350°F. Mash the potatoes, add the onion, eggplant, sea salt, and chili powder. Then form the mixture into patties. Put the patties on oiled baking sheets and sprinkle each one with a little oil. Bake them in the oven for 30 minutes until they are golden brown. Serve them hot or cold with salads and horseradish.

SUGAR SNAP PEAS

My favorite way to eat sugar snap peas is raw, or possibly with some hummus, but if you are going to cook them, I like this recipe best.

50 mL oil give or take 20 mL
a few cloves of garlic, peeled and thinly sliced
50 mL tamari sauce
mushrooms, optional
sugar snap peas, washed and tips removed
onions, sliced into rings - optional
bell pepper, sliced into thin strips - optional
ginger root, sliced into thin strips - optional
basil, - optional
tahini - optional

Heat a cast iron skillet or other heavy frying pan. Add the oil. When the oil is hot, add the garlic. Stir vigorously so that the garlic doesn't burn. When the garlic is brown, add the tamari sauce and mushrooms, if using. When the mushrooms are cooked, add the onions. When the onions are cooked, add the bell pepper, or any other ingredients if using. When everything is cooked, toss in the sugar snap peas. Turn off the heat but leave in the pan until the sugar snap peas turn bright green. Add a tablespoon or so of tahini, if using, just before serving.

SAVORY SQUASH TART
winter squash
chili
salt
onion
thyme
soy milk

Combine cooked and pureed squash with a dash of red chili powder and salt, onions that have been sauteed with thyme and enough soy milk to form a soupy consistency. Bake the custard (acorn squash, onions sauteed with thyme, enough soy milk to make it the consistency of unbaked pumpkin pie filling, a dash of red chili powder and sea salt). When the custard is done, I will spoon it into the crust and when it cools, we should have a savory acorn squash tart.

TOFU SCRAMBLE - GREEK STYLE

A description of the way portulaca oleracea is prepared in Greece inspired this delicious recipe!
peanut oil
portulaca oleracea, roughly chopped
three whole peeled tomatoes (canned with basil)
salt
tofu

Start with a generous circle of oil in the middle of a large cast iron skillet and put the stove on medium high heat. Saute the portulaca oleracea. Add a package of extra firm tofu, one crushing fistful at a time so it has the consistency of scrambled eggs, going into the pan. Add the three tomatoes, breaking them up so tomato juice thoroughly soaks the tofu, then add salt to taste.

SIMPLE YUMMY TOFU SCRAMBLE

When Elena was almost one, we invited a few friends and neighbors over on President's Day for a semi spontaneous brunch. We served this tofu scramble with steamed asparagus, chili onions and a drizzle of roasted pumpkin seed oil. Everyone agreed it hit the spot!

oil, enough for form a pool in the center of your pan
turmeric, roughly a teaspoon
brown mustard seeds, roughly 1 ½ teaspoons
fenugreek, roughly ½ teaspoon
tofu, 2 pounds
sea salt, roughly ½ teaspoon

Heat large cast iron skillet over medium high heat. Add oil. When the oil is warm, add ground turmeric, fenugreek, brown mustard seeds and salt. When the spices bloom, add the tofu, one crushing fistful at a time so it has the consistency of scrambled eggs, going into the pan. Alternatively, before heating the pan, you can drain the tofu and add the drained tofu to the hot spice infused oil at this stage, mashing it with a spoon to give it the consistency of scrambled eggs. Serve warm. Store any leftovers in an airtight dish and eat them as you would enjoy egg salad.

TOSTADAS

I didn't think to write this as a recipe but my husband noted that it's not an automatic dish from many people. So...

cooked beans – enough for 1 serving per person. If your person is a tiny toddler, a serving might be ¼ cup, if your person is like my over 6ft tall brother-in-law, your serving might be 2 cups
tomatoes, chopped
lettuce, rolled and sliced on a bias so you have long strips
tortillas, ½ to 2 per serving per person

Place the tortilla on the plate – if you are using corn tortillas, toast them or fry them in oil before plating them. Cover the tortilla with cooked beans, mashed or not, black or pinto. Cover the beans with shredded lettuce and chopped tomatoes. Enjoy either by picking up the crispy tortilla, or by cutting off bite sized pieces with your fork if you are using flour tortillas.

7 CURRIES, SOUPS, AND STEWS

THAI CURRY SAUCE
2 Tablespoons oil (either a neutral oil like sunflower or safflower or a strong oil such as sesame or peanut)

1 teaspoon of curry paste (yellow, green, red or musamun)

1 can premium coconut milk.

Heat oil in sauce pan on high heat. Add curry paste of your choice and stir fry for 1 to 2 minutes, until the paste is bubbling. Add coconut milk and bring to a boil. Remove from heat immediately and pour over cooked rice or vegetables.

GREEN CURRY PASTE
1 clove garlic

1 small/medium yellow onion

2 thumb sized pieces of ginger root

4 stalks lemon grass

1 teaspoon new mexico dried green chili powder

rind from 1/2 a lime

1 teaspoon ground coriander

1 teaspoon ground cumin

2 tablespoons sunflower

1 tablespoon agave nectar

1 tablespoon tamari sauce

Combine all ingredients in a food processor - keeps in the fridge, in a glass container for several months.

GREEN CURRY (TOFU)
2 tablespoons sunflower oil
1 teaspoon green curry paste
canned bamboo shoots
canned baby corn
1 medium onion
baby bok choi
1 package firm tofu
2 tablespoons tamari
1 teaspoon agave
1 can premium coconut milk
1 can water (to cover the vegetables)
fresh basil (garnish)
Put the oil and paste in a pan on high heat and stir until the paste is bubbling. Add the rest of the ingredients and cook until bok choi is tender.

GREEN CURRY VARIATION
2 tablespoons sunflower oil
1 teaspoon green curry paste
canned bamboo shoots
canned water chestnuts
1 medium onion
broccoli florets
green onions, chopped
1 package firm tofu
2 tablespoons tamari
1 teaspoon agave
1 can premium coconut milk
1 can water (to cover the vegetables)
fresh thai basil (garnish)
Put the oil and paste in a pan on high heat and stir until the paste is bubbling. Add the rest of the ingredients and cook until broccoli is tender.

GREEN CURRY VARIATION I
2 tablespoons sunflower oil
1 teaspoon green curry paste
canned bamboo shoots
canned water chestnuts
1 medium onion
red bell pepper
broccoli florets
1 package firm tofu
3 green onions

8 snow peas, snapped in ½
2 tablespoons tamari
1 teaspoon agave
1 can premium coconut milk
1 can water (to cover the vegetables)
fresh thai basil (garnish)

Put the oil and paste in a pan on high heat and stir until the paste is bubbling. Add the rest of the ingredients, except the snow peas and green onions. Cook until broccoli is tender. Remove from heat and add the green onions, snow peas and basil. Serve immediately!

INDIAN INSPIRED CURRY
2 teaspoons ground ginger
1 ½ teaspoons ground coriander
¾ teaspoons ground cumin
¼ teaspoons turmeric
oil
leek, chopped
bell pepper, sliced
1 pound tofu, cubed
1 can coconut milk
equal amount crushed tomatoes
1 teaspoon salt

Put oil in a sauce pan and let the spices bloom. Add leek. When the leek is tender add the remaining ingredients. Reduce to a simmer until ready to serve.

MUSAMUN CURRY PASTE

20-30 large red chili peppers, dried
2 stalks fresh lemon grass
1 shallot
5 cloves garlic
1 thumb sized piece of ginger root
zest from an organic lime
10 stems of cilantro
1 tablespoon coriander seeds
1 teaspoon cumin seeds
1 teaspoon salt
½ ground cinnamon
1 teaspoon agave
½ teaspoon tamari
2 tablespoon sunflower oil
soak peppers for 5 minutes

Put all ingredients in a 2 inch deep dish and roast at 350 for 15-20 minutes, then combine all ingredients in a food processor. Store in a glass jar with a tight lid in the fridge for up to several months

MUSAMUN CURRY (TOFU)

2 tablespoons sunflower oil
1 teaspoon regular curry paste
2 medium zucchini
1 small eggplant
1 medium yellow onion
2 carrots
1 package firm tofu
2 tablespoons tamari
1 teaspoon agave
1 can premium coconut milk
1 can water (to cover the vegetables)

Put the oil and paste in a pan on high heat and stir until the paste is bubbling. Add the rest of the ingredients and cook until the eggplant is tender.

RED CURRY PASTE

15-20 red chili peppers, seeded
2 stalks of lemon grass
1 clove garlic
1 tablespoon chopped ginger
3 kafir lime leaves, chopped
¼ cup cilantro root, chopped

1 teaspoon salt or tamari sauce

½ teaspoon ground coriander seeds

½ teaspoon ground caraway seeds

2 tablespoons sunflower oil

Combine all ingredients in a food processor - keeps in the fridge, in a glass container for several months

YELLOW CURRY PASTE

Browsing cookbooks in Barnes and Noble, I came across Keo's Thai Cuisine which contained the first recipe I had every seen for Yellow Curry Paste. Of course, we had to purchase it and it was the inspiration for the following recipe.

3 cloves garlic

1 hot green chili pepper (small)

1 rocket sized onion

a thumb sized piece of ginger root

2 stalks of lemon grass

1 teaspoon salt

1 teaspoon ground coriander

1 teaspoon brown mustard seeds

1 teaspoon red chili powder

1 teaspoon turmeric

¼ teaspoon cinnamon

2 tablespoons sunflower oil

1 tablespoon agave nectar

combine all ingredients in a food processor - keeps in the fridge, in a glass container for several months

YELLOW CURRY (TOFU)

The first time I ever had yellow curry, was in Los Angeles. I dubiously ordered it because my mother told me it was good and nothing else on the menu that was appealing. I loved it! After we moved away, whenever we visited the first thing we would do when we arrived and the last thing we did before we left was to order yellow curry. I have had yellow curry in many other restaurants but this only served to reinforce that when I want yellow curry, I want the one they serve at the Vegan House in LA. It's the perfect blend of sweet and hot deliciousness! Now that I know how to make yellow curry paste, I make myself yellow curry whenever I am hungry for it and don't need to first purchase a plane ticket to Los Angeles.

2 tablespoons sunflower oil
1 teaspoon yellow curry paste
2 medium red potatoes
1 medium yellow onion
2 carrots
1 package firm tofu
2 tablespoons tamari
1 teaspoon agave
1 can premium coconut milk
1 can water (to cover the vegetables)

Put the oil and paste in a pan on high heat and stir until the paste is bubbling. Add the rest of the ingredients and cook until the potatoes are tender.

SOUPS

ALPHABET SOUP

Who doesn't like minestrone soup? Especially when the noodles are in the shape of alphabets letters?

1 onion
1 leek
some baby bock choi
scallions
dried basil
1 can whole peeled tomatoes with basil
4 cups pinto beans, cooked
vegetable alphabets (Eden organics)

Boil alphabet noodles. While noodles are cooking, saute onions, chopped vegetables, tomatoes, and basil. When noodles are cooked, add tomato mixture to pot of noodles and noodle water. Add pinto beans, salt and serve.

ASPARAGUS SOUP

My served this soup to me when I visited her with my one month old daughter. When I tried to make it at home, it was not very appetizing. It turns out the secret is to pour in the olive oil while the blender is running and keep pouring until you see or hear a slight change indicating a change of texture. That will make this soup creamy and velvety.

asparagus
olive oil
salt
water

Snap the ends off each asparagus. Steam the bottoms you have snapped off separately from the rest of the asparagus spear. Put most of the asparagus spears in the blender with olive oil and salt, reserving a few tips per bowl of soup to use as a garnish. Blend the cooked bottoms in a blender and run them through a food mill to remove the woody bits. Enjoy! It makes a lovely appetizer or a light, refreshing spring dinner.

AVGOLEMONO SOUP

I have no idea how this soup compares to the Greek egg and lemon soup. But I've been intrigued by the idea of a vegan avgolemono soup for years and something resembling this soup appeared by the name in a raw food book. I didn't like the author's recipes, but this soup is delightful, yellow and creamy. I served it one night when attempting a raw food meal inspired by Moroccan cuisine and everyone wanted the recipe.

3 cups warm water
1 teaspoon saffron threads
1 jicama
2-4 cups soaked raw cashews
juice from one lemon
olive oil to taste
1 teaspoon sea salt (more to taste if desired)

Soak the cashews for 4-8 hours at room temperature or overnight in the fridge. Warm the water and add the saffron. Combine the jicama, lemon and cashews in the food processor until smooth. Transfer the saffron water and cashew jicama mixture to a soup tureen. Add the salt and olive oil and serve with mushroom gravy.

GREEN BORSCHT

The idea for this soup came from a recipe that my Russian teacher had called "summer borscht." Her recipe was noticeably lacking in beets and produced a green colored soup but that is the only resemblance to this recipe.

1-2 onions, sliced
1-2 potatoes, cubed
about 3 cups water
spinach
about 1 ½ teaspoons salt
cooked noodles
oil

Saute onions. Add the cubed potatoes and enough water to cover the vegetables. Add salt to taste. Let simmer until the potato is tender, then add the spinach and cooked noodles.

BUTTERNUT SQUASH SOUP

This is a lovely quick soup on a fall or winter evening when you have cooked winter squash on hand. I typically use butternut squash as it's my favorite, but any winter squash will do.

serves 2
2 tablespoons fat
1 onion, minced
1 stalk of celery
3-4 fresh sage leaves, finely chopped
2 cups cooked, pureed butternut squash
salt to taste
1 tablespoon red chili powder

Saute the onion. Add celery and sage leaves. When well cooked, add the butternut squash, chili and salt. Serve warm.

BUTTERNUT SQUASH SOUP VARIATION

My favorite spices for butternut squash are sage, nutmeg and chili. It turns out my husband is not a fan of nutmeg in his winter squash so I do not make this variation when I'm making soup for him. I will perhaps add some ginger, or use any of the pumpkin soup recipes or variations, using butternut squash instead of pumpkin, but this is a lovely soup if he is not joining us for soup and, again, it has the advantage of being quick!

2 tablespoons fat
6 clumps of fresh sage leaves
¾ teaspoon garahm masala
1 package frozen butternut squash

Saute the sage leaves. Add the butternut squash and garahm masala.

Serve when the butternut squash is warm throughout.

CREAM OF COCONUT SOUP

I made this one evening after discussing the perfect carrot soup with my husband. This is simple, elegant and sure to please. The first time I made this I used a variety of carrots that are naturally white so the soup had a beautiful ivory color. The blending at the end is optional and this is quite tasty with spinach and onions.

sesame oil

4-7 carrots, enough to half fill a 6 quart stock pot when thinly sliced

7 cups water

1 teaspoon ginger

salt to taste

toasted chili powder to taste

1 can premium coconut milk

Heat a 6 quart stock pot over medium heat. Add sesame oil (enough to generously cover the bottom). When the oil is warm, reduce to low heat and begin adding the sliced carrots. I used a hand held mandolin over the stock pot and sliced carrots until my baby needed my attention which was after I had managed to fill about half the pot. When the carrots have been added, add 7 cups of water. This should just cover the carrots. If it doesn't, adjust your other ingredients accordingly. That is, add more water or more carrots or even better, continue following the recipe with the amounts you have to make a soup that won't have the exact taste or consistency of the soup I describe here but that will still be quite tasty. Bring the water to a boil, then reduce to low heat and simmer until the carrots are cooked. I nursed the baby for about 45 minutes the first time I made this soup. When the carrots are tender, add salt, coconut milk, chili powder and ginger and put everything in a blender until creamy. Since my blender holds seven cups and this soup recipe makes roughly twice that, I found it was best to blend in batches. This recipe, with freshly baked bread, was a hearty dinner for 5 people. If I remember correctly, it made 10-12 bowls of soup. Everyone had seconds and some people had thirds.

FALL CARROT SOUP
1 bunch of celery, roughly chopped
2 pounds carrots
1 butternut squash, roasted
salt to taste
2 teaspoons paprika
1 nutmeg, grated
½ teaspoon ground ginger
sunflower oil
8 cups filtered water
roasted pumpkin seed oil

Wash and slice the carrots, celery and set aside in separate bowls. Heat the soup pot on medium high. Once the pot is warm, add the oil. When the oil is hot, add the paprika, nutmeg and ginger; stir continuously. When the spices bloom (smell nice), add the carrots. Stir briskly and when the carrots begin to be tender, add the chopped celery. Add the water and turn the heat up. When the water boils, reduce to a simmer and add (a teaspoon) salt. When the aroma fills the house, add the butternut squash. Taste for salt content. Add more salt if necessary. Put the soup in a blender, or use a hand held blender or pour the soup through a sieve (retaining the stock) and mash the contents of the sieve before recombining it with the stock. This will give the soup a creamy consistency. Serve with bread and a salad, and garnish with roasted pumpkin seed oil.

CUCUMBER SOUP
onion
coconut oil
water
cucumber
salt

Mince a fresh spring onion and saute the bulb in a tablespoon of coconut oil, before adding the tops. When the tops are cooked enough that they no longer have a strong bite, but raw enough that they were still bright green, add the water or vegetable stock. Let the water onion mixture warm up over low heat while grating a large cucumber. When the water is no longer cold, remove it from the low heat, stir in the cucumber, add a pinch of salt and enjoy!

DAHL MIDDLE EASTERN STYLE
Once when Andrew and I were moving, I was hungry for a bowl of soup. The only vegetarian choice at the restaurant where we were eating was red lentil. When I ordered it, it was much thinner, and had a very different flavor from the red lentil soup that comes out of my mother's

kitchen. I notice the large party of East Indians at the table next to us had also ordered the soup, so I asked them what they thought. They all agreed that it could stand more lentils, more spices and less water. An older gentleman commented, "In India, this is what we serve to invalids." That give you a sense of the heartiness of this soup. It is not a one dish wonder, but it can sometime be very nice along side rice, salad, falafel, etc. when you have a large crowd and are interested in creating a feast!

2 cups red lentils
½ teaspoon salt
½ teaspoon ground coriander
6 cups water
fresh lemon

Rinse lentils three times in cold water. Put everything in a medium sized pressure cooker. Bring to high pressure, then cool in cold water to depressurize and serve immediately. Squeeze lemon over each individual serving bowl.

MINESTRONE SOUP
pinto beans, cooked
noodles, cooked (rigatoni or trumpet are my favorite)
tomatoes
basil
oregano
salt
sauteed onions (one yellow, one red)
chopped broccoli
carrot (optional)
bell pepper (optional)

Saute the onions, carrots and bell peppers. Add the beans, tomatoes, noodles and spices. When thoroughly heated, add the chopped broccoli. Cook until the broccoli is tender, but still bright green. Remove from heat and drizzle with olive oil.

MINESTRONE SOUP VARIATION
pinto beans, cooked
noodles, cooked (rigatoni or trumpet are my favorite)
canned tomatoes
basil
thyme
red chili powder
salt
leek
thinly sliced zucchini
olive oil

Wash, slice and saute the leek with dried basil, thyme, salt and chili. While it is cooking, thinly slice the zucchini and add them to the leek. When the zucchini is aldente, add the beans, tomatoes, noodles. When thoroughly heated remove from heat and drizzle with olive oil.

MISO SOUP
2 tablespoons of dried wakame
3 pieces of kombu
1 bunch of baby spring/green onions
½ cup (approx) of red miso paste
sesame oil
filtered water

Set the wakame and kombu to soak in separate bowls of filtered water. While the seaweed is soaking, slice the green onions, separating bulbs from leaves. After the seaweed has been soaking for 10 minutes, drain the water and replace with fresh filtered water. Saute the onion bulbs in sesame oil. Then add the drained, chopped kombu (this is why soaking it is key). After the kombu has had a chance to blend flavors with the onion bulbs, add the chopped onion leaves. Once the leaves are cooked, the wakame should have been soaking for a total of 20 minutes; add it to the pot. Combine the miso paste with water and pour this into the soup, remove from heat and enjoy!

MISO SOUP VARIATION (serves 2)
½ yellow onion
4-6 stalks of celery
½ bunch of parsley
½ bunch of spinach
½ package firm tofu
1 tablespoon sunflower oil
4-8 tablespoon red miso paste*
filtered water

What to do: Slice the onions and celery, cube the tofu and tear the parsley and spinach into bite sized pieces. Put the sunflower oil in the bottom of a medium sized sauce pan over high heat. Add the sliced onions. When they begin to change texture, add the celery. When the celery begin to change texture, add the tofu, parsley and spinach. When the onions and celery are cooked to the desired texture, remove them from heat. Combine the miso paste with with some filtered water to form a smooth broth. Add this to the sauce pan and serve immediately.

*red miso paste has a richer flavor than yellow or white miso. It can be found in the refrigerated section of health food store, frequently next to the tofu.

NAIL SOUP

This soup does not actually call for a nail. Like the soup in the children's story, Nail Soup, is made with anything you have on hand. The important part is the technique. Start with a large stock pot. Put oil on the bottom of the pot, as much as an inch and saute any aromatics you have on hand such as onion, garlic, shallots, leeks or celery root, herbs, salt. When the aromatics soften, add the hard vegetables such as potatoes and carrots. If not using potatoes or carrots, add as much water as you want soup and any vegetables such as broccoli, summer squash, peas. Bring the water to a boil and then reduce it to a simmer until the vegetables turn bright green. Just before serving the soup, add any leafy greens you are using such as celery, baby bock choi, kale, spinach, parsley. The heat of the soup will cook them sufficiently.

FRENCH ONION SOUP

I had always been curious about french onion soup, but never tasted it or attempted it because every recipe I ever came across called for beef, or at the very least, bullion cubes. It wasn't until I was in my thirties that I read some french man's opinion that authentic french onion soup has only onions, oil and water. No recipe was attached to this opinion but it gave me the courage to make the soup described below. My husband loved it and declared it to be the best french onion soup he's ever eaten. It's only disadvantage is that it requires quite a bit of time. I have not found a shortcut that is also vegan.

Serves 6

onions

oil

water

Thinly slice 5 onions. Stir sliced onions into several tablespoons of hot oil with ½ teaspoon salt over medium high heat. Cover and cook until the onions are wet and slightly wilted, about 10 minutes. Uncover and continue to cook, stirring occasionally, until the liquid cooks off and the onions are translucent, about 20 minutes. Reduce the heat to low and continue to cook frequently scraping brown bits on the bottom of the pot, until deep brown and very soft, 40-60 minutes. Continue to cook the onions, stirring only once every 5 minutes so that a dark crust covers the bottom of the pot, about 10 minutes. Stir in ¼ cup water and scrape up the crust, continuing to cook until another dark crust forms, about 2-3 minutes. Repeat this process 2 more times. Stir in 6-8 cups of water and let simmer for 10 minutes. Serve with melted cheese or hot bread.

FRENCH ONION SOUP FOR TWO

One night in early spring, I was hungry for French Onion soup, but it was only my husband and I at dinner that night and I didn't want soup for the next week so this is what I did.

1 and ½ large red onions

oil

water

Thinly slice the onions. Heat sunflower oil in the bottom of a sauce pan. Add sliced onions to hot oil. Add ¼ teaspoon coarse salt and cook over medium high heat. Stir somewhat frequently until the onions are wet and slightly wilted. Continue to cook, stirring occasionally, until the liquid cooks off and the onions are translucent. Reduce the heat to medium low and leave them alone until brown bits form on the bottom of the pot. Scrape them off with a wooden spoon and repeat, until all are deep brown and very soft. Continue to cook the onions, stirring only once a dark crust covers the bottom of the pot. Add 2 tablespoons water and scrape up the crust. Continue to cook until another dark crust forms. Add 2 tablespoons water and scrape up the crust. Continue to cook until another dark crust forms. Add 2 tablespoons water and scrape up the crust. Continue to cook until another dark crust forms. Add 2 tablespoons water and scrape up the crust. Continue to cook until another dark crust forms. Add 2 cups of water let simmer. I added 3 cups, but it was slightly watery and we had 1 cup left over so I think it would have been better if I had only added two cups.

CORINNA'S POTATO SOUP

I remember my grandmother washing and chopping the potatoes for this soup while watching The Price is Right and supervising my efforts to make an Ojo de Dios. Every time she made this soup it was delicious. I think her secret was the fine chopping of each ingredient. She had a saying that onions should be tasted, not seen!

1-2 onions, minced

2-3 carrots, quartered and then thinly sliced

7-8 potatoes, cubed

salt

pepper

1 tablespoon toasted flour

Wash and then finely chop all the vegetables. Put the oil in the bottom of your pot and turn the heat on medium to high. When the oil is hot, add the onions and stir continuously. When the onions start to look cooked, add the carrots, followed by the potatoes. Stir constantly so that nothing sticks to the pan. At this point add the salt, pepper, and water. While the soup is cooking, toast the flour. Once the flour is toasted, add water a little at a time to form a roux. When the potatoes are tender, add the roux and serve.

HEARTY POTATO SOUP
8 potatoes, cubed
1 small celery root (optional)
1 onion, chopped
1 carrot, optional
salt and red chili flakes to taste
dried basil
dried parsley
2 tablespoons sunflower oil
filtered water
green onion, chopped

Wash and then finely chop all the vegetables. Put the oil in the bottom of your pot and turn the heat on medium to high. When the oil is hot, add the onions and stir continuously. When the onions start to look cooked, add the carrot, followed by the celery root, if using. Add the potatoes. Stir constantly so that nothing sticks to the pan. At this point add the salt and dried herbs. When the potatoes are half way cooked, (they are thoroughly cooked when they are soft) add filtered water, approximately 6 cups. Taste for salt content. Add more if necessary. When all the root vegetables are tender, put the soup in a blender, or use a hand held blender or pour the soup through a sieve (retaining the stock) and mash the contents of the sieve before recombining it with the stock. This will give the soup a creamy consistency. If a thicker consistency is desired, toast some flour in a dry pan and then combine the flour with a little liquid from the soup to form a roux, adding this to the soup. Serve with chopped green onion and red chili flakes and bread.

MOTHER'S POTATO SOUP
1-2 onions
2-3 carrots
7-8 potatoes
salt
dried basil or red chili powder
1 tablespoon toasted flour

Wash and then finely chop all the vegetables. Put the oil in the bottom of your pot and turn the heat on medium to high. When the oil is hot, add the onions and stir continuously. When the onions start to look cooked, add the carrots, followed by the potatoes. Stir constantly so that nothing sticks to the pan. At this point add the salt, dried basil or red chili powder, and water. While the soup is cooking, toast the flour. Once the flour is toasted, add water a little at a time to form a roux. When the potatoes are tender, add the roux and serve.

POTATO SOUP

4 potatoes
1 small celery root
1 onion
2 carrots
salt to taste
4 tablespoons dried basil
1 teaspoon dried oregano
2 tablespoons sunflower oil
filtered water

Wash and then finely chop all the vegetables. Put the oil in the bottom of your pot and turn the heat on medium to high. When the oil is hot, add the onions and stir continuously. When the onions start to look cooked, add the carrots, the celery root and the potatoes. Stir constantly so that nothing sticks to the pan. At this point add the salt and dried herbs. When the carrots are half way cooked, (they are thoroughly cooked when they are soft like a cooked potato) add filtered water, approximately 6 cups. Taste for salt content. Add more if necessary. When all the root vegetables are tender, put the soup in a blender, or use a hand held blender or pour the soup through a sieve (retaining the stock) and mash the contents of the sieve before recombining it with the stock. This will give the soup a creamy consistency.

POTATO SOUP VARIATION

2 onions
5-6 potatoes
2 teaspoons salt
1 tablespoon dried basil
2 teaspoons oregano
2 tablespoons flour
½ pound green beans, broken into thirds or fourths

Saute onions and potatoes. Add water and boil. Toast flour. Add broth to toasted flour in a blender. Add to soup with green beans. Serve.

PUMPKIN SOUP
1 large yellow onion
3 tablespoons sunflower oil
6 cups cooked, pureed pumpkin
2 cups water
6-8 fresh sage leaves
4 tablespoons butter or oil
½ of a nutmeg, grated (½ - 1 teaspoon ground nutmeg)
1 teaspoon salt (or to taste)
Slice onion into rings and saute in oil. Add pumpkin & water to onions. In a separate skillet, melt butter or warm oil. Add sage and cook for 5 minutes. Mix sage into soup. Add spice. Heat and Serve.

PUMPKIN ACORN SQUASH SOUP
1 large red onion, minced
3 stalks celery, sliced
3 tablespoons sunflower oil
1 small pie pumpkin cooked, pureed
1 acorn squash cooked, pureed
water
6-8 fresh sage leaves, chopped
1 ½ teaspoon nutmeg, grated
salt to taste
chili powder to taste
Saute onion and celery in sunflower oil. Add sage leaves, then pumpkin, acorn squash and water. Add spices. Serve.

PUMPKIN SOUP VARIATION
minced onions
salt
chili powder
ground ginger
freshly grated nutmeg
pumpkin pulp
filtered water
Saute onions. Add salt and spices, except nutmeg. Add pumpkin and water. Grate nutmeg freshly over each individual serving. Mmm...pumpkin soup.

PURPLE SOUP
My high school chemistry teacher was coming over for lunch in about 20 minutes. I had neglected to go grocery shopping. My meeting with my thesis adviser had run over and I just had time to get home, stash my book

bag and see what I could pull together. My fridge had assorted condiments, a package of tofu, purple cabbage, a purple onion, some fresh basil and some snow peas. In the pantry were some canned bamboo shoots, water chestnuts and thankfully some coconut milk. I decided to put together the following soup and it was not only remarkably good, but it was also a delicate lavender color that made it especially appealing visually!

1 red onion, sliced
oil
4-8 leave purple cabbage, sliced into thin (¼ inch) strips
3-6 snow peas
1 can coconut milk
1 can bamboo shoots
1 can water chestnuts
1 package tofu, cubed
salt
3 bunches of thai basil, chopped

Saute onion with salt. Then, one at a time, add bamboo shoots, water chestnuts, tofu, and cabbage, letting each addition cook and begin to soften before adding the next. When the cabbage is wilted, add the coconut milk. Once the coconut milk is warm, toss in the washed snow peas, remove from heat. Add the basil and serve immediately.

SALAD SOUP

I first made this one spring when getting over a winter cold. The original version has the top of 1 leek, 5 stalks of celery, the last 8-10 leaves of a head of romaine lettuce, ½ a bag of baby lettuces, 1 bag of baby spinach, ¾ package of sprouts, ¼ a bunch of parsley, roughly a teaspoon of himalayan rock salt. It was so delicious, I immediately wrote down what I did and shared it with my sister. Most recently, I put kale instead of spinach. This added a bitter note I wasn't fond of and wasn't as robust as the version with spinach.

green leek tops, well washed
celery stalks, well washed
parsley greens, gently washed
romaine lettuce, mixed baby greens, spinach, alfalfa sprouts – whatever you have on hand that is green -
salt and lemon

Put salt and greens in a stock pot with water, then bring to a boil. Reduce to a simmer until the greens float to the bottom. Serve with a squeeze of fresh lemon in each bowl. - Good for a general spring cleanse.

FAVORITE SUMMER SOUP

Years after writing this recipe, I wondered why I called it my favorite "summer" soup when all the ingredients are clearly available in the fall, winter and spring and many summer recipes call for ingredients that just aren't available year round. I later realized it was because it requires so little cooking that I appreciated it one summer. This could plausibly be renamed "quick winter soup." Whenever you eat it, enjoy!

2-3 onions
1 celery root
¼ ginger root
1 teaspoon salt
spinach, chopped
6-10 tablespoons red miso paste

Saute the onions, celery root and ginger. Add water and salt. When the celery root is tender, add the spinach and red miso paste. Serves 3-5.

DELIGHTFUL TOMATO BASIL SOUP

1 large onion or 2 small onions either yellow, white or red
2-3 tablespoons sunflower or safflower oil
3.5 cups crushed tomatoes (about 15-35 washed fresh tomatoes – depending on size)
1 bunch chopped basil
2-5 bell peppers sliced or finely chopped (optional)
Salt to taste
Olive oil to taste

Saute the onions followed by the bell peppers if adding them in the sunflower or safflower oil. Add the tomatoes and basil (if dried). When the tomatoes are thoroughly heated, but before the soup begins to boil, remove from heat and blend to puree any onions and bell peppers that weren't finely chopped. After blending, add the fresh basil chopped, reserving several leaves for garnishing each bowl of soup. Drizzle olive oil over each serving or add fresh organic mozzarella cheese. If you are serving this soup with cheese or fresh organic cream, do not serve any carbohydrates with the meal. Simply enjoy the soup with a nice salad and possibly some carrot juice

SIMPLE TOMATO SOUP

2 tablespoons fat
1 clove garlic
1 can whole peeled tomatoes with basil
salt
1 small bunch, small leaf basil, chopped
10 fresh oregano leaves, chopped

Saute the garlic. When the garlic is tender and fragrant, add the tomatoes, salt and herbs. Serve warm with fresh cheese, cooked pasta or bread.

SPRING/SUMMER TOMATO BASIL SOUP (serves 2)

½ onion

2 bell peppers

1 bunch asparagus

½ bunch spinach

6 cups crushed tomatoes (canned from last year will be better than not yet super ripe hot house grown tomatoes from this year)

1 tablespoon dried basil

1 teaspoon dried oregano

1 tablespoon sunflower oil

Slice the onions and bell peppers. Saute them in sunflower oil, break the asparagus into bite sized pieces and add to the sauteed onion and pepper. Tear the spinach into bite sized pieces and add it to the soup. When the spinach is wilted, add the tomatoes and dried herbs. When the soup is thoroughly warm, remove from heat and garnish with goat cheese or olive oil. My favorite way to eat this soup is with sliced cucumber or with a salad.

THAI GINGER SOUP

I first had a thai ginger soup as part of the lunch special at Thai Orchid in Albuquerque, New Mexico. It was delicious, but I couldn't figure out what all the flavors were. After many different recipes and experiments I settled on this version of Thai Ginger Soup which works with *Zingiber officinale*, the ginger most readily available in the United States, but is spectacular when made with fresh kha, *Alpinia galanga*. I prefer to use the common ginger root rather than canned or jarred kha if fresh kha is not available. When kha is canned or jarred, it is typically pickled which adds an unpleasantly sour note to the soup. Recently I have noticed dried kha sold under the name "galangal root." If you have dried kha, put it in the coconut milk and water at the outset along with the fresh lemon grass so that the flavor has a chance to be extracted from the dried root. I also adore this soup with fresh lemon grass cut into one inch stalks, but when fresh lemon grass is unavailable, it is preferable to use lime juice than to use frozen, canned, jarred or dried lemon grass. The preserved versions of lemon grass just don't hit the spot for this delicately flavored soup. While it was tricky to track down what ingredients would reproduce the soup I loved so well, the most surprising part of this recipe to me was the technique which I gleaned from a recipe for chicken soup in Keo's Thai Cuisine.

1 package tofu
3 cups coconut milk
2 cups water
1 inch section kha (Thai Ginger)
3 tablespoons tamari sauce
lemon grass
¼ cup fresh lime juice
2 tablespoons sliced green onions
1 tablespoon cilantro

Cut tofu into thin strips. Bring coconut milk and water, lemon grass and dried kha (if unable to attain fresh) to a boil. Reduce heat to medium low; add tofu and cook for about 3 minutes. Stir in ginger, tamari sauce and lime juice. Sprinkle with green onions, cilantro and serve hot!

VEGETABLE NOODLE SOUP
Make Nail Soup. Add cooked noodles. Enjoy.

VEGAN VICHYSSOISE

I had never been very interested in vichyssoise because the ingredients all seemed to be potatoes, leeks, salt, pepper and cream – boring – especially if you omit the cream. Then one day I was reading a book set in France where the character's mother-in-law made "leeks" for the toddlers and they adored them. I did a little research and discovered that French recipes for leeks, almost universally (I have never seen one that didn't, but am not willing to say categorically that none exist) call for a potato to be added. So one day, I had left over mashed potatoes and the white parts of some leeks (I had used the green parts for Salad Soup) and I made the following soup. Upon later testing I made it with whole leeks and for it just as satisfying.

2 potatoes per person
½ leek per person
salt to taste
nm red chili powder to taste
oil for sauteing the leeks
water
mimi-cream (a product that a friend shared with me over figgy pudding one Christmas) – optional

Boil the potatoes until well cooked or use left over mashed potatoes. Finely chop the leeks. Saute them in the pot you wish to make the soup in. When the leeks are cooked, add the cooked potatoes. Put everything in a blender with water from cooking the potatoes, or fresh water if you are using left over potatoes, and blend until creamy – a few seconds. Add salt and chili to taste. In individual portions add mimicream, if desired.

BASIC WINTER SOUP
1 potato, cubed
4 carrots, thinly sliced
3 stalks of celery
salt
chili powder
oil

Put oil in a stock pot on medium heat. Add the potatoes, then the carrots, one at a time. Add celery and enough water to cover the vegetables. Add salt and chili to taste. Simmer until the potato is tender. Serve hot.

WINTER CARROT SOUP

1 red onion

1 red bell pepper

5 pounds carrots

1 pound butternut squash (I used the organic frozen cubed butternut squash)

salt to taste

1 tablespoon red chili powder

6 fresh sage leaves

2 tablespoons sunflower oil or European style organic butter

filtered water

Wash the carrots, then finely chop the red onion, and the bell pepper. Put the butter or oil in the bottom of your pot and turn the heat on medium to high. When the oil is hot, add the onions and stir continuously. When the onions start to look cooked, add the bell pepper, stir briskly, reduce the heat to low and begin thinly slicing the carrots, adding them to the soup as you slice them. When all the carrots have been added, turn the heat up and resume stirring constantly so that nothing sticks to the pan. At this point add (a teaspoon) salt, the chopped sage leaves and the red chili powder. When the carrots are half way cooked, (they are thoroughly cooked when they are soft like a cooked potato) add the butternut squash. If the butternut squash is raw, peel and chop it before adding it to the soup. If the butternut squash is already cooked, wait to add it until the carrots are cooked. When the carrots are cooked, add filtered water to achieve the desired consistency. I add approximately 6 cups. If you add too much, cooking the soup on low heat will create a tasty reduction. Taste for salt content. Add more if necessary. Put the soup in a blender, or use a hand held blender or pour the soup through a sieve (retaining the stock) and mash the contents of the sieve before recombining it with the stock. This will give the soup a creamy consistency. Serve with bread and a salad, or if no carbohydrates are served with the soup and one is not vegan, fresh organic cream can be used as a garnish.

WINTER ROOT VEGETABLE SOUP

4 potatoes

1 small celery root

1 leek

1 yellow onion

6 carrots

2 parsnips

1 bunch parsley

salt and red chili powder to taste

4 tablespoons dried basil

1 teaspoon dried dill
2 tablespoons sunflower oil
filtered water

Wash and then finely chop all the vegetables. Put the oil in the bottom of your pot and turn the heat on medium to high. When the oil is hot, add the onions and stir continuously. When the onions start to look cooked, add the carrots, followed by the leek, the celery roots, the potatoes and parsnips. Stir constantly so that nothing sticks to the pan. At this point add the salt, red chili powder and dried herbs. When the carrots are half way cooked, (they are thoroughly cooked when they are soft like a cooked potato) add filtered water, approximately 6 cups. Taste for salt content. Add more if necessary. When all the root vegetables are tender, put the soup in a blender, or use a hand held blender or pour the soup through a sieve (retaining the stock) and mash the contents of the sieve before recombining it with the stock. This will give the soup a creamy consistency. Serve with chopped parsley, bread and a salad.

STEWS

AUNT AURORA'S BEANS

My aunt Aurora makes the best beans. I love to eat her beans. Whenever we went over to her house, she would make us beans sometimes with fried potatoes, sometimes with calabacitas. One day I asked her how she made them. "Oh it's just beans and water, and once they're cooked a little salt. Nothing fancy. If you have chicos, you can put those in. I like to add a little ham, but no – you're vegetarian. You wouldn't eat ham." So I went home and made them. They did not taste like aunt Aurora's beans. So the next time I asked her, "What exactly do you do to make beans? I want to know every little step. Don't leave anything out!" and this is the recipe she gave me.

2 cups dried beans, washed

6 cups filtered water

½ teaspoon salt

Take the dried beans and spread them out on the table to look for any rocks. Once you know they are just beans, removed any that are broken, shriveled or rust colored. Then take the beans a handful at a time and blow on them as you move them back and forth from hand to hand to get the dust off. Transfer them from hand to hand 3-4 times before setting them in a bowl and getting the next handful. Once all the beans are in a bowl, fill the bowl with cold water and swish the beans around. Transfer the beans to another bowl to continue washing them. Take your pressure cooker or stock pot and using your first bowl, put three times as much water as beans in your pot. Cover it and turn the stove to high so the water can heat while you wash the beans. "The secret to good beans Mama used to say was to always cook them in hot water. If you need to add more water to the pot to keep them from scorching, you heat the water to boiling and then you add it. Cold water in the beans makes them tough." Mama, of course, referred to her mother, Elena Gonzalez, my great grandmother. Once the water is heating, fill the bowl of beans with water, swish them around and scoop them out of the water into a clean bowl. Do this until the water is clear – three to seven times. Place the dried beans in the pot of hot water. Bring to high pressure than reduce to low heat for 1.5 hours if you are using a pressure cooker at sea level. If you are using a stock pot it will take about four hours. Times will be even longer at higher altitudes. The beans are done when they are tender and can be salted and then served.

CHICOS AND BEANS

Chicos are sun dried corn kernels and can be purchased online. It seems this dish was made by Algonquin Indians in New England and the colonists renamed it succotash.

at least 1 cup dried pinto beans, washed

¼ cup chicos

at least twice as much water as beans

salt

After the beans are washed, put them in a pressure cooker with three times as much water as beans, by volume, chicos, salt and cook for 1.5 hours. When the beans are tender, they are ready to eat.

COSTA RICA STYLE BLACK BEANS

When we went to Costa Rica for the first time and wanted to make beans, we discovered they didn't have hot chili or tamari sauce but they invariably used oregano and lime juice in preparing frijoles. I was skeptical since I don't like beans with garlic and mother never put oregano or lime in her beans at home, but they were good and now when I make them, I remember the feeling of being in Costa Rica.

at least 1 cup dried black beans, washed

water

onion

tomato

oregano

salt

lime juice

After the black beans are washed, put them in a pressure cooker with three times as much water as beans, by volume. Add a whole onion, peeled and with the root removed, 1-5 tomatoes, depending on size and fondness for tomatoes, salt, dried oregano and cook for 1.5 hours. When the beans are tender, serve them with a squeeze of lime juice in each bowl.

BASIC DAHL

My friend Prakash told me that if I ladled it over rice, it would be just like the Biryani his mother in India makes.

2 cups red lentils

½ teaspoon ground ginger

½ teaspoon red chili powder

½ teaspoon salt

½ teaspoon ground turmeric

4 cups water

Rinse lentils three times in cold water. Put everything in a medium sized pressure cooker. Bring to high pressure, then cool in cold water to depressurize and serve immediately.

DAHL VARIATION

My mother frequently made this in the winter in New Mexico with a side of flour tortillas or cornbread. I am a lazy cook and simplified it to the recipe found above. You can, of course, make this in a pressure cooker, or make the recipe above in a sauce pan if you don't have a pressure cooker. The difference between these two is the vegetables and the texture and flavor change that occur when you saute the red lentils before adding water. I like this technique with brown rice. Having eaten it without this step for some years, I now prefer the version above. My mother vehemently disagrees with me on this point, and we get to see how tastes diverge over time.

2 cups red lentils
1 thumb length of ginger root, julianned (optional)
1 teaspoon red chili powder
½ teaspoon salt
½ teaspoon ground turmeric
1 small onion, minced or sliced
1 carrot, quartered and thinly sliced
broccoli, spinach, or any other desired vegetable
sunflower or safflower oil
4 cups water

Rinse lentils three times in cold water. Put a small spoonful of oil in the pot. Saute onion, carrot and ginger root. Add the rinsed lentils and mix well. Add salt, chili, turmeric and water. Cook over medium heat until the lentils soften (about 40 minutes). Just before removing from the heat, add the broccoli, spinach, baby bok choi, kale, or other desired vegetable. Fish out ginger root (this is mandatory if you have used ginger in this recipe because the ginger flavor intensifies over time and even 20 minutes makes an enormous impact on the final flavor) and serve. The heat from the cooked dahl will lightly steam the vegetables you have just added leaving them bright green and slightly crunchy rather than greyish green and mushy. If you leave the ginger root in the dahl, the ginger flavor will intensify over time. Even an hour's time produces a noticeable increase in ginger flavor. This is desirable if the dahl is for someone getting over a cold or other illness where ginger would be beneficial.

SAVORY KUGELESQUE DISH

When we first went to the Grand Canyon as a family, my mother only had on pot and one burner on her camping stove, so she decided to cook the noodles with the potato soup instead of cooking them separately like she usually did. When she did that, the starch from the noodles stayed in the soup, rather than being discarded and turned the potato noodle soup into a thick stew that you could stand a spoon upright in when it cooled.

We loved it and asked her what it was called, so she said, "Rugelach!" and that's what we called it. But rugelach isn't a stew, it's a pastry! So when I was writing this cookbook, I assumed I must have misremembered and the only german sounding name that looked like something even close to what this dish is was Kugel. Hence the name here.

1-2 onions
1-2 carrots
3 potatoes
salt
4 cups water
uncooked noodles

Saute the onions, followed by the carrots and potatoes. Add the salt, water and noodles, so that the noodles cook in the water of the soup. The starch from the cooking noodles will give this dish a kugelesque consistency.

LENTIL SOUP

This soup was a staple of my diet one California winter in San Francisco. It was quick, easy and filling. This is still my favorite lentil soup.

2 cups lentils
1 teaspoon salt
1 tablespoon dried basil
1 teaspoon oregano or thyme
1 can whole peeled tomatoes with basil
1 can measure of water

Combine all the ingredients in a pressure cooker. Bring to high pressure for 3-5 minutes. Let cool on it's own. Garnish each bowl with a drizzle of olive oil.

LENTIL BARLEY SOUP

The winter the above soup was a staple of my diet, I would sometimes vary it by adding barley, depending on my mood. When I served it to my Aunt Aurora one lunch with some fresh bread, she commented that I added too much barley. "Barley is expensive!" She said, "You can just put a little for flavor. You don't have to put so much. The lentils are good to eat as a soup." I don't know where or when barley was expensive, but when I'm making this soup, I use a generous hand.

2 cups lentils
½ -1 cup barley
1 teaspoon salt
1 tablespoon dried basil
1 teaspoon oregano or thyme
1 can whole peeled tomatoes with basil
1 can measure of water

Combine all the ingredients in a pressure cooker. Bring to high pressure for 3-5 minutes. Let cool on it's own. Garnish each bowl with a drizzle of olive oil.

GREEN LENTIL STEW

Green lentils are actually light brown, olive, or tan in appearance. This delightfully hearty soup hits the spot on a winter day.

2 onions
3 potatoes
6 carrots
¼ cup dried basil
1 tablespoon salt
4 cups lentils
several tablespoons oil
water
2 pounds crushed tomatoes with basil

Put oil in a pan. Saute onions, carrots, potatoes, lentils, salt, basil. When toasted, add 2 cans crushed tomatoes with basil and water. Cook until the lentils are tender.

SPLIT PEA SOUP

"Some like it hot! Some like it cold! Some like it in the pot nine days old!" I always think of split pea soup when I hear that rhyme. I don't like it hot. I don't like it cold. I don't like it in the pot nine days old, but I do like serving a bowl while it is hot and letting it cool to room temperature before eating it. As the soup cools, the texture changes. It thickens and even will take the shape of the bowl it is served in if sufficiently cool.

onion

carrots
split peas
water
salt
thyme (optional)

Saute the onions, chopped carrots, and split peas. Start with the onions and add the carrots when the onions start to smell good and and the raw split peas after the carrots have had a chance to begin cooking (about 2 minutes). Once the split peas are toasty, add the water so that there are 2 inches of water above the peas. Seal the pan tightly and the soup will take about 40 minutes. If your pan does not have a tight seal you may need to add more water during the cooking process and it may take as long as an hour and a half for the peas to become tender. Add the salt and thyme (if using) at the end of the cooking process as adding the salt at the beginning can slow down the cooking process. I like to enjoy this soup with a nice cornbread or herbed biscuits.

SIMPLE SPLIT PEA SOUP

One afternoon I was reading a story about a princess in exile who didn't know how to cook and was given a few dried peas and instructed to boil them. In the story she lamented the absence of salt and an herb or two. I was curious, so I boiled split peas with a little salt and a pinch of thyme. It was delicious!

split peas
water
salt
thyme (optional)

Place all ingredients in a pot over low heat. Sometime later (a long time – the princess in the story put the peas in the pot over the coals before falling asleep and ate the result in the morning) enjoy the soup.

8 DELIGHTFUL DINNERS

FLAVORS OF THE MIDDLE EAST

BABA GANOUSH FOR A PARTY OF FORTY
4 large eggplants, roasted
1 cup lemon juice (3-6 lemons)
4 cloves garlic, peeled and minced
1 cup tahini paste (available at whole foods next to the almond butter)
1 teaspoon salt
high quality olive oil to taste
3 teaspoons red chili powder (optional)

To roast the eggplant, pierce each eggplant with a fork (so the steam can escape as they roast) and bake at 350 for approximately 35 minutes. Check them at 20 minutes. They should be soft everywhere so that you can scoop the eggplant out of its skin. Put the roasted eggplant in the food processor or blender with all the other ingredients except the olive oil. You may need to break this into 4 or more batches, depending on the size of your kitchen equipment. Pulse until everything is combined into a smooth paste. Transfer to a serving dish and immediately before serving, cover with a layer of olive oil (9-12 tablespoons - so yes - a lot!). As people serve themselves, the olive oil mixes with the eggplant dip and the taste explodes in your mouth. If you incorporate the olive oil at the beginning or omit it entirely, the dip tastes flat.

FALAFEL
In Feast from the Middle-East, Faye Levy notes that canned chickpeas, which are already cooked, are not a good substitute for the dried ones, as a falafel mixture made from them would be too soft, but on the next page she says "There is no need to soak the chickpeas; simply use canned ones."

Her dry bean recipe calls for stale bread, baking powder and flour. Her canned bean recipe calls for breadcrumbs and eggs. We have not found that falafel patties need any of these ingredients. Our recipe is:

2 cups of dried garbanzo beans
2 cloves of garlic
½ a small onion
½ a bunch of parsley
½ teaspoon salt
1 generous teaspoon cumin
1 ½ teaspoon coriander
½ teaspoon new mexico red chili powder (optional)

Place the garbanzo beans in a small serving bowl and cover with water for approximately 8 hours. Refrigerate the garbanzos (water and all) if you do not use them within 12 hours of having begun to soak them. Put the garlic in the food processor to mince it. Then add the onion and parsley. Transfer to a bowl and add the garbanzos to the food processor in batches, so that a nice dough is formed and there are no whole or partial chickpeas Transfer to a bowl. Add cumin, salt, coriander and chili (if using) and mix well. When the mixture is well blended, take 1 tablespoon of mixture and form it into a flat patty. Saute each patty in a frying pan, adding oil as needed to prevent patties from sticking. The patties will need to be flipped so that each side is cooked. Serve with tzadiki sauce, babaganoush or hummus.

TZADZIKI SAUCE
vegan mayonnaise
dill
parsley (optional)
garlic (optional)
onion (optional)

What to do: chop all the ingredients finely (I put them all in the food processor and about 10 seconds later it's done) and then stir them into the vegan mayonnaise If I am just adding dill to veganaise, there is no need to involve a food processor. A simple spoon will suffice.

GREEN GARLIC HUMMUS

Green garlic has a more delicate flavor than dried garlic and is not as antagonistic to someone sensitive to member of the lily family. I love to make this dish is spring when the green garlic is first popping up and I would like a hummus that has some flavor, but not the overpowering garlic taste and bitterness that can sometimes accompany dried garlic.

1 can chick peas/garbanzo beans

1/3 cup lemon juice (1-2 lemons)

3-4 green garlic shoots or 1 big clove, peeled, (as opposed to a head) of garlic

¼ teaspoon salt

3 tablespoons olive oil

1 teaspoon red chili powder

If you want to make a dip, drain the liquid from the canned beans and put it in the blender. - If you want to make a soup, put canned beans and the liquid they were canned in with the other ingredients in the blender and buzz until smooth.

HUMMUS

I was a college student; my friend had a recipe from a magazine that she wanted to try. Armed with the relevant ingredients and a blender, we made this new and strange dish called hummus. Since the magazine version we used called for half a bunch of parsley, it was bright green! It was delicious. I decided to make this delightful dish from scratch because everyone knows that dried beans you have cooked yourself are much tastier and healthier for you than canned beans. A few hours after putting the garbanzo beans on to cook, the entire dorm was filled with the most terrible stench. Further inquiry determined it was the garbanzo beans I was making. That was when I realized that it's not that I like garbanzo beans, (which we never had at home) but that I like the combination of garlic, lemon juice and olive oil so much, I am even willing to eat garbanzo beans! Since then, I have made hummus many times, writing down the results of my experiments to hit just the right notes. Too much or too little garlic, lemon, olive oil or salt make a passable, but unimpressive dip. The combination of ingredients below reliably deliver a remarkable hummus. You can, of course, use dried chick peas that you cook, but to this day I do not appreciate the smell of cooking garbanzo beans and keeping a few cans on hand at all times is convenient and insures that I have something to whip up at a moments notice.

1 can chick peas/garbanzo beans

1/3 cup lemon juice (1-2 lemons)

3-4 green garlic shoots or 1 big clove, peeled, (as opposed to a head) of garlic

¼ teaspoon salt

3 tablespoons olive oil
1 teaspoon red chili powder

Mince the garlic in the food processor. Drain the liquid from the canned beans and add them along with the lemon juice and salt. Spoon the spread into your serving dish. Sprinkle with chili powder and drizzle the olive oil over the top. As people eat the hummus, the olive oil gets incorporated with the other ingredients.

PARSLEY HUMMUS VARIATION
2 cans organic chickpeas
juice from 1 lemon
1 teaspoon salt
½ teaspoon New Mexico red chili powder, mild (optional)
half a bunch of fresh parsley (optional)
2 cloves garlic
generous tablespoon of tahini (optional)
olive oil

Mince the garlic and finely chop the parsley. Blend everything to a paste. Serve with a sprinkling of olive oil.

KASHKE BADEMJAN (without the kashke)
At waiter once suggested this at an Iranian restaurant and we had to order it because of the name. Leaving out the kashke makes it vegan. It is quite a tasty dish and kashke is apparently difficult to acquire if you do eat dairy.

1 large eggplant, roasted
1 small onion, minced
1 medium garlic clove, minced
1 teaspoon fresh peppermint or a small dash of dried peppermint

Roast the eggplant. When the eggplant is cooked, set it aside to cool and heat oil in a cast iron skillet. Add the onion. When the onion is half browned, add the garlic; then add the mint. Put the cooled eggplant in the food processor. Transfer to a serving dish and add the onion, garlic, mint mixture.

LENTILS (Iranian Style)

I first had this at a restaurant in Palo Alto when we were house hunting in preparation for our move from Pasadena to the Stanford area. An Indian family dining at a table nearby, also new to that dining establishment, commented that it reminded them of the lentil soup they feed someone who is ill because it lacks all hot spices.

2 cups red lentils

½ teaspoon ground cumin

½ teaspoon salt

4 cups water

Rinse lentils three times in cold water. Put everything in a medium sized pressure cooker. Bring to high pressure, then cool in cold water to depressurize and serve immediately with a squeeze of fresh lemon juice. This makes a feast when paired with saffron rice, and a meze platter.

TABOULI

Mix

1 cup bulgar wheat, rinsed in cold water

3 bunches parsley

1 bunch green onions

1 ½ lemon, juiced

½ cup olive oil

garden mint, optional

let stand for at least 20 minutes to let the flavors marinate before serving.

TABOULI SALAD FOR A PARTY OF FORTY

2 cups bulgar wheat

4 bunches parsley

2 bunches green onions

1 bunch fresh peppermint

5 small or 3 large tomatoes

4 cucumbers

juice of 4-6 lemons

¼ - 1 cup olive oil

Rinse the bulgar wheat in filtered water and then soak it in just enough water to cover to the wheat for 6 hours. After the wheat has absorbed all the water and has a soft consistency rather than a hard/crunchy consistency, mince the parsley, green onions, peppermint, tomatoes, cucumbers. Combine everything in a serving dish and enjoy!

ZA'ATAR
2 parts ground sumac
2 parts dried thyme
1 part sesame seeds

PASTA, PIZZA, POLENTA

THE BEST EVAR!!!

There have been pestos I've enjoyed and pestos I haven't really cared for. One summer in CA, we had so much basil, I was making pesto on a regular basis. When I made the recipe below, it was so delightful I wrote down what I had just done and it makes a reliably delicious pesto every time!

1 bunch basil
½ teaspoon salt
2 med cloves garlic
10-20 stems of parsley
approximately 2/3 cup pine nuts
a generous handful of arugula
olive oil

Pulse garlic in the food processor with salt. This insures the garlic is minced and the salt evenly distributed so you don't end up with one bite that has too much garlic or too much salt. Add parsley next. The parsley gives this a beautiful green color. Add pine nuts. If you add them too early, it will be hard to make sure everything is smoothly incorporated and no one likes to find a mouthful of parsley stem, garlic or salt. Add alternate handfuls of basil and arugula. Transfer immediately to a glass container. Seal the top with olive oil immediately to prevent the basil from oxidizing and turning black. I frequently cover mine with up to an inch or so of olive oil replacing the olive oil as I use it so that the top layer is always protected from air. refrigerate until using.

THE BEST PESTO EVAR VARIATION

I like this even better than the original version because this recipe has so much flavor, the pine nuts in the original provide more texture than flavor, as the sunflower seeds do here and organic sunflower seeds are less than two dollars a pound while organic pine nuts are more than seventeen dollars a pound.

1 bunch basil
½ teaspoon salt
20 stems of parsley
2/3 cup sunflower seeds
a generous handful of arugula
olive oil

Pulse the sunflower seeds in the food processor with salt. Add parsley. Add basil and arugula. Transfer immediately to a glass container. Cover with olive oil. refrigerate until using.

MAI FUN NOODLES
Mai Fun noodles, cooked
onion, sliced
whole peeled tomatoes with basil, canned
fresh chopped basil
½ teaspoon salt
½ teaspoon dried thyme
  cook Mai Fun Noodles (rice vermicelli) according to directions on the package. Caramelize an onion. Add a can of whole peeled tomatoes with basil. Add fresh chopped basil, salt, dried thyme and serve over mai-fun noodles.

FRESH PASTA
This recipe came from my friend's Italian grandmother and is the only one I've ever encountered that doesn't call for eggs.
  Sift
1 cup of flour per person
Add water, working vigorously until dough is smooth and firm. Divide into 10 pieces. Roll each piece. Divide again. Roll again until cylinders are as thick as a pencil. Cook in abundant boiling water until aldente.

HERBED PASTA
Cook four servings of your favorite pasta. After draining it, add enough olive oil so that it doesn't stick. Toss it with one of the following herb combinations:
  1 tablespoon dried basil, 1 ½ teaspoon dried oregano, ½ teaspoon salt;
  1 ½ teaspoon dried basil, 1 ½ teaspoon dried oregano, ½ teaspoon salt;
  2 tablespoons each of Mexican oregano, red chili seeds or flakes, ½ teaspoon salt;
  2 tablespoons fresh thyme, chopped and 1 tablespoon dried basil, 1 teaspoon salt;
  4 sprigs fresh basil chopped and 1 tablespoon dried parsley;
  1 tablespoon each red chili flakes and ground dried rosemary, 1 teaspoon salt.

RAW PASTA
zucchini, thinly sliced lengthwise
black olives
grape tomatoes
2 cups sunflower seeds
water
1 jar sun dried tomatoes packed in olive oil

Put the zucchini through a pasta maker or slice with a knife to make fettuccine style "noodles." Put sunflower seeds the the food processor with a jar of sun dried tomatoes and pulse until a paste is achieved. Add enough water to achieve the consistency of a tomato creme sauce. Toss with zucchini, olives and grape tomatoes. Serve immediately!

PASTA VARIATIONS

When making pasta, think about the way the topping will combine texturally with the pasta. I like to use bow tie, spiral, penne, or trumpet pasta when serving it with a sauteed vegetables mix to toss over the pasta. I prefer to use angel hair, capelini or spaghetti when serving pasta with herbs. Pasta with sauce can be lovely too! I love to eat spaghetti with marinara sauce or fettuccine with a white sauce. When I am baking pastas, I like to use penne or lasagna noodles. Pasta is such a versatile dish. It is a carbohydrate that combines with leafy vegetables and herbs. The body has trouble digesting it properly when combined with proteins or sweets but in and of itself, or with a leafy green salad, it is a wonderful dinner.

PASTA WITH VEGETABLES

While the pasta is cooking, saute the vegetables. I begin with the most firm to the most delicate and add one vegetable to the saute at a time, letting each vegetable begin to cook before adding the next. Favorite combinations are:

artichoke hearts, lemon juice, parsley;

carrots, broccoli, yellow squash, asparagus, bell pepper, tomatoes, snow peas, olive oil;

carrots, broccoli, yellow squash, mushrooms, asparagus, bell pepper, tomatoes, snow peas, olive oil;

eggplant, tomato, basil;

eggplant, tomato, basil, thyme, rosemary;

fresh tomato, fresh basil;

fresh tomato, fresh basil, green onions

Pasta with Vegetables continued...

fresh tomato, red chili flakes, salt;

fresh tomato, red chili flakes, garlic

fresh tomatoes, green garlic, salt;

145

garlic, tomato;

garlic, olives, tomato, red chili flakes

leeks, red, white, green onions, parsley, salt;

onions, Japanese eggplant, bell pepper, mushrooms, dried basil, parsley, chili, salt, fresh tomato;

onions, Japanese eggplant, bell pepper, mushrooms, dried basil, parsley, chili, salt, olives, fresh tomato;

white onion, minced, crimini mushrooms, thinly sliced, red chili flakes, ground dried rosemary, salt;

onions, asparagus, tomatoes, snow peas, fresh basil, dried oregano, olive oil, salt;

onion, butternut squash, sage, salt;

onion, butternut squash, celery, chili, ginger, sage, salt;

onion, butternut squash, fresh sage leaves sauteed in olive oil;

onion, green bell peppers;

onion, green bell peppers, basil, salt;

onion, bell peppers, mushrooms, basil, salt;

onions, squash blossoms, salt;

onions, eggplant, tomato, basil, (rosemary) (thyme)

onion, spinach, red chili flakes, salt;

onion, spinach, tomato, red chili flakes, salt;

red onion, tomatoes,arugula, salt;

oyster mushroom, green onions, olive oil;

All of these dishes are made with pasta and vegetables and opposed to pasta and sauce.

PARTY PASTA

Cook bow tie, spiral, penne or trumpet pasta normally. As soon as it has been drained toss in olive oil, raw snow peas and cherry tomatoes, halved, chopped green onion, 12-20 leaves fresh basil, chopped, 1 tablespoon dried oregano, 1 teaspoon salt. The heat from the pasta will cook the peas and tomatoes to perfection. Serve immediately, garnishing with a few whole leaves of fresh basil.

TOMATO "CREME" SAUCE

2 cups sunflower seeds

1 jar sun dried tomatoes packed in olive oil

water

Put sunflower seeds the the food processor with a jar of sun dried tomatoes and pulse until a paste is achieved. Add enough water to achieve the consistency of a tomato creme sauce.

BAKED PASTA
cooked pasta
olive oil
yellow onion
spinach
salt
tofu
basil
salt
red onion
tomatoes
basil
oregano

Drain 4 servings of cooked noodles (lasagna noodles or penne work very well – I buy the pasta made from Jerusalem artichokes)

Add 2 tablespoons olive oil to the cooked pasta while still hot.

Saute 1 yellow onion with one bunch of spinach and a pinch of sea salt.

Blend one package of firm organic tofu with 3 tablespoons dried basil and salt to taste

Saute 1 red onion in 2 tablespoons olive oil and add crushed tomatoes with basil and fresh chopped oregano.

Place the pasta in the bottom of a casserole dish and layer with pureed tofu, spinach and marinara sauce.

Bake at 350 for an hour

SUMMER PASTA
fettuccine pasta
fresh broccoli
tomatoes
snow peas
bell peppers
onion

While the pasta is cooking, lightly saute the vegetables beginning with the onion, then the peppers then the broccoli. When the broccoli is tender and bright green (before it turns yellow from overcooking) remove the vegetables from the heat. Toss over cooked pasta with olive oil, salt, red chili, and the uncooked snow peas and tomatoes. The heat from the pasta will cook the peas and tomatoes to perfection. Serve immediately.

RAW PIZZA
raw cracker or bread
marinara
cashew cream

greens

To make pizza, put the marinara sauce on your raw bread of choice and top with cashew cream and micro greens.

PIZZA

Andrew made his special sauce, put it on some hamburger buns, topped them with the "ricotta cheese" I made from soaked cashews, lemon juice and salt ala Cafe Gratitude and put it in the oven at 350 for a few minutes (until the cashew "cheese" began to subtly change color) and then topped it with roasted red bell peppers and the "Brazil Nut Parmesan Cheese" (also from Cafe Gratitude's I am Grateful cookbook). It was *super* yum! We both enjoyed it a lot.

PIZZA VARIATIONS

marinara sauce, onions, spinach, bell peppers, olives, mushrooms, green onions;

pesto sauce, onions, fresh tomatoes, mushrooms, bell peppers, olives

fresh basil, fresh tomatoes, green peppers, fresh parsley;

WHO NEEDS CHEESE VEGETABLE PIZZA

For most of my life it seemed like cheese less pizza was missing something. My mom is vegan so if we ever went to Upper Crust Pizzeria, she would always order a pizza with no cheese, and even adding salt, though it made it better, did not make it satisfying. When I first had the pizza at Cafe Gratitude in Berkeley CA it was the essence of good pizza which led to a phase of making cashew cheese for pizza. My mother pointed out that the cashew cheese combined with the pizza crust violates the rules of proper food combining but if I was going to eat pizza, I wanted it to have cheese, even if the cheese was made from cashew nuts. And then I had this pizza. And it was delicious. And after four pieces, I realized it didn't have cheese or cheese substitute and I didn't miss it. The second or third time I made it, Andrew – mr connoisseur of cheese pizza himself – had one that was just tomatoes and declared it good. This pizza recipe has become my pizza of choice and like a good cheese pizza, I think it is even more delicious cold for lunch the next day.

onions
red or yellow bell peppers
fresh tomatoes (optional)
spinach (optional)
eggplant (optional)
zucchini (optional)
mushrooms (optional)

Make your favorite pizza crust and your favorite pizza sauce. Saute each vegetable topping separately in plenty of olive oil and a little salt with the exception of the tomatoes and the spinach. Wilt the spinach and slice the tomatoes if using. Decorate your pizza with as many or as few topping as you wish. Bake as the pizza dough recipe instructs.

ANDREW'S FAVORITE "FAST FOOD"

any available bread
tomato sauce (can be as simple as a can of crushed tomatoes with basil and a little salt added)
any cheese
dried oregano

Completely cover bread with sauce and cheese. Melt cheese under broiler. Sprinkle dried oregano on top and serve.

Some of the ingredients in this section may be unfamiliar. Heart of palm can typically be found in the canned goods section near the canned artichoke hearts. Chicos, corn husks, green chili powder, red chili powder, and chili pequin can all be ordered from Los Chileros de Nuevo Mexico. We always use the New Mexico Red Chili Powder, mild because it has a beautifully mellow flavor that is sometimes sacrificed for heat in their hotter versions.

ARROZ CON PALMITO (VACA MUCA STYLE)

When my husband and I visited my mother in Costa Rica, we took a day to see the Arenal volcano and the La Fortuna waterfall. For dinner that evening, we went to a restaurant called Vaca Muca and I ordered their rice with heart of palm dish. The recipe bellow is my recreation of that meal when I returned to the states.

cooked rice
heart of palm
red bell pepper
oregano
olive oil
sea salt
onion

Warm olive oil in a skillet. saute heart of palm (sliced), onion and bell pepper. Add rice. eat with Costa Rican style black beans and fried plantains.

AUNT AURORA'S BEANS

My aunt Aurora makes the best beans. I love to eat her beans. Whenever we went over to her house, she would make us beans sometimes with fried potatoes, sometimes with calabacitas. One day I asked her how she made them. "Oh it's just beans and water, and once they're cooked a little salt. Nothing fancy. If you have chicos, you can put those in. I like to add a little ham, but no – you're vegetarian. You wouldn't eat ham." So I went home and made them. They did not taste like aunt Aurora's beans. So the next time I asked her, "What exactly do you do to make beans? I want to know every little step. Don't leave anything out!" and this is the recipe she gave me.

2 cups dried beans, washed
6 cups filtered water
½ teaspoon salt

Take the dried beans and spread them out on the table to look for any rocks. Once you know they are just beans, removed any that are broken, shriveled or rust colored. Then take the beans a handful at a time and blow on them as you move them back and forth from hand to hand to get the dust off. Transfer them from hand to hand 3-4 times before setting them in a bowl and getting the next handful. Once all the beans are in a bowl, fill the bowl with cold water and swish the beans around. Transfer the beans to another bowl to continue washing them. Take your pressure cooker or stock pot and using your first bowl, put three times as much water as beans in your pot. Cover it and turn the stove to high so the water can heat while you wash the beans. "The secret to good beans Mama used to say was to always cook them in hot water. If you need to add more water to the pot to keep them from scorching, you heat the water to boiling and then you add it. Cold water in the beans makes them tough." Mama, of course, referred to her mother, Elena Gonzalez, my great grandmother. Once the water is heating, fill the bowl of beans with water, swish them around and scoop them out of the water into a clean bowl. Do this until the water is clear – three to seven times. Place the dried beans in the pot of hot water. Bring to high pressure than reduce to low heat for 1.5 hours if you are using a pressure cooker at sea level. If you are using a stock pot it will take about four hours. Times will be even longer at higher altitudes. The beans are done when they are tender and can be salted and then served.

CHICOS AND BEANS
Chicos are sun dried corn kernels and can be purchased online. It seems this dish was made by Algonquin Indians in New England and the colonists renamed it succotash.

at least 1 cup dried pinto beans, washed
¼ cup chicos
at least twice as much water as beans
salt

After the beans are washed, put them in a pressure cooker with three times as much water as beans, by volume, chicos, salt and cook for 1.5 hours. When the beans are tender, they are ready to eat.

COSTA RICA STYLE BLACK BEANS
When we went to Costa Rica for the first time and wanted to make beans, we discovered they didn't have hot chili or tamari sauce but they invariably used oregano and lime juice in preparing frijoles. I was skeptical since I don't like beans with garlic and mother never put oregano or lime in her beans at home, but they were good and now when I make them, I remember the feeling of being in Costa Rica.

at least 1 cup dried black beans, washed
water
onion
tomato

oregano
salt
lime juice

After the black beans are washed, put them in a pressure cooker with three times as much water as beans, by volume. Add a whole onion, peeled and with the root removed, 1-5 tomatoes, depending on size and fondness for tomatoes, salt, dried oregano and cook for 1.5 hours. When the beans are tender, serve them with a squeeze of lime juice in each bowl.

MAMA'S BEANS

These are the beans I remember my mother making when I was growing up.

at least 1 cup dried pinto or anasazi beans, washed
water
tomato and onion
powdered ginger root
salt
tamari sauce
oil
chili pequin, optional

After the beans are washed, put them in a pressure cooker with three times as much water as beans, by volume. Add a tablespoon or so of oil, a whole onion, peeled and with the root removed, 1-5 tomatoes, depending on size and fondness for tomatoes, salt, a pinch of ginger, a splash of tamari sauce and cook for 1.5 hours. When the beans are tender, serve them as they are or with a sprinkling of chili in each bowl.

BEAN BURRITO

tortilla or chapati
refried beans
lettuce, chopped
fresh tomato, chopped

Spread the tortilla or chapati with refried beans. Cover with lettuce and tomato. Roll up and enjoy!

BREAKFAST BURRITO

2 cooked potatoes (I used baked potatoes left over from the night before)
1 bell pepper
1 onion
sunflower oil
basil
sea salt
whole wheat tortillas
salsa

Slice the onion and dice the bell pepper. Saute the onion, adding the bell pepper and the potatoes. When everything is well cooked, add basil (I used one bunch of fresh basil, but 1-4 tablespoons dried basil works equally well), salt, and spoon it onto a tortilla and enjoy with fresh salsa.

LUNCH BURRITO

3 baby zucchini
½ package frozen corn
1 onion
cooked beans (whole or mashed)
sunflower oil
sea salt
whole wheat tortillas
salsa

Slice the onion and zucchini. Saute the onion, adding the zucchini and the frozen corn. When everything is well cooked, spoon it onto a tortilla along with the cooked beans and enjoy with fresh salsa.

DINNER BURRITO

1 package firm tofu
1 bunch green onions
1 portabello mushroom
dried basil
tamari sauce (a wheat free soy sauce)

Slice the onions and mushrooms. Cut the tofu into cubes. Put the sunflower oil in a seasoned cast iron skillet and turn the heat on high. After 35-60 seconds (give the oil a chance to heat up), add the sliced onions. When the onions begin to change color/texture, add the mushrooms. When the mushrooms begin to change color/texture, add the tofu, and tamari sauce; stir gently so as not to break the tofu. When the tofu has absorbed the flavor, spoon it into a tortilla and cover with dried basil.

EL PATIO BURRITO

I whipped out the red chile sauce I made last night when I was hungry for my grandmother's boiled potatoes in chile, heated up some beans (with onion, ginger, and soy sauce, of course), put the beans in the tortilla rolled it with the ends on the bottom (just like they do at El Patio), covered it with the chile gravy, sliced some pepper jack thinly on top and popped it in the oven on broil until the cheese melted - mmm, mmmm... It was even better than El Patio's and it was all organic. and I didn't have to worry about forgetting to request a whole wheat tortilla, and I wasn't tempted by the nasty white flour sopapilla that I always think will taste good but that in fact never tastes good and almost always makes my stomach ache!

ENCHILADAS

Make a red chili sauce. Put red chili powder and flour in a dry skillet. Turn the heat on high and stir constantly. When the smell of the chili and toasting flour fills the kitchen but before it begins to darken, transfer to a sauce pan with 2 tablespoons oil and add water. Cook the sauce over medium heat (warm enough to form little bubbles, cool enough not to be a roiling boil) stirring constantly (to prevent formation of lumps) until the sauce begins to thicken. If the sauce is beginning to thicken and there are still some lumps, you can pour it into a blender and buzz it a few times to get the lumps out. Add salt to taste before pouring the sauce over anything. The ratio of chili powder to flour will affect the heat of the finished sauce. To start out I use 4 tablespoons red chili, 4 tablespoons flour, 4 cups water, 2 tablespoons sunflower oil, 1 teaspoon salt. If the sauce is too hot, the next time I will use 2 tablespoons chili and 6 tablespoons flour. If it is not hot enough I might use 6 tablespoons red chili powder and 2 tablespoons flour. The gluten in the flour is what causes the sauce to thicken.

While cooking the sauce, toast a dozen corn tortillas in the oven until they are crispy. Chop an onion finely. When the red chili is ready, put a corn tortilla in the red chili sauce then grab another tortilla and use it to catch any chili that drips from the first tortilla as you transfer it from the sauce to the baking dish you are using to make the enchilada. Putting the tortillas in the sauce with cause them to soften. This is why you want them crisp initially. If they curl while toasting, no problem. Once you put them in the sauce they will unfurl. Layer the tortillas in the bottom of the baking dish, putting a layer of chopped raw onion just under the top layer of tortillas. Bake in the oven at 350 for 20-30 minutes.

GALLO PINTO

In Costa Rica, they say it's not a meal unless it includes rice and beans. The rice and beans are referred to as "Gallo Pinto." To make gallo pinto, you take cooked rice and cooked black beans and heat them in a frying pan with some oil until the dish is warm and the rice has absorbed the bean juice taking on a speckled hue. This dish can have onion, carrots, heart of palm, bell pepper or any other vegetable that you might cook with rice, but the essentials are rice and beans.

FRIED POTATOES

Fried potatoes and refried beans are my preferred side dish to accompany enchiladas, burritos, tamales, or tofu scramble. They are delicious for breakfast with red chili sauce or rolled into a tortilla with salsa as a breakfast burrito.

cooked potatoes
onions, cut into slivers or diced
oil
salt to taste
chili powder to taste, optional

In a skillet or pan, heat the oil. Add the onion. Cook until the onion is tender. If the potatoes are whole, cut them at least, in half. I like to cut them into bite sized pieces, though large chunks also work. The smaller the potato, the greater the exposed surface area which will brown nicely. The larger the potato, often, the less work. Once the onion is tender add the potatoes and cook until brown. Add salt and chili, if desired.

DUSHENKA'S NOT- HOT SALSA

I came up with this when I first started dating my now husband who was born on Long Island, NY and completely unaccustomed to any food with any hint of heat. I wanted to enjoy chips and salsa with him and this recipe works.

1 can whole peeled tomatoes with basil
juice from 1 lemon
4-7 sprigs parsley; 2 sprigs small leaf basil
3 green onions

Salt to taste. Chop herbs and onions finely. Mix all ingredients in a medium sized bowl. Enjoy with tortilla chips.

SALSA FRESCA

I am not a fan of cilantro. And, occasionally I am hungry for a salsa fresca I ate once at a friends house that included cilantro.

chopped tomatoes
chopped green onion

chopped hot pepper
lemon juice
salt to taste
1 can whole peeled tomatoes

RANCHOS SALSA

In San Diego there is a vegan organic mexican restaurant called Ranchos. My mother took me there when my sister moved there in February and I was so enamored with their food that my sister would call me and ask when I was coming back for a visit because she was feeling hungry for Ranchos. When I went to San Diego for my brother's wedding, I realized that my beans are better, my potatoes are better, my calabacitas are better, my tamales and enchiladas are infinitely better... In fact, I like everything they serve better when I make it in my own kitchen with the exception of their salsa. Their salsa is the best salsa I've ever had, and being raised in New Mexico, I have eaten quite a bit of salsa in my day. When I returned to New England from my brother's wedding, I was already missing Ranchos salsa on the plane ride home. Luckily for me, I returned during a glut of fresh ripe tomatoes and perfect pepper and abundant onions. All of this led me to recreating Rancho's salsa, or at least, a salsa that is exactly what I want to eat when I want salsa.

ripe tomatoes (several large)
green onions (scallions)
green raw annaheim pepper
lemon juice
salt

Put all the vegetables in the blender and liquify them. Add lemon juice and salt to taste. When I first did this, hoping to recreate Ranchos salsa, I was disappointed that instead of the salsa I was hoping for, what I created was a spicy v-8 or bloody mary mix. Yuck! Luckily I needed to go do something else and decided to toss it into a mason jar and refrigerate it until I could figure out what to do with it. The next day, I realized the "juice" had separated in the pulpy part (which looked and tasted like what they serve at Ranchos for salsa) and a clear liquid. I don't know how long this keeps in the fridge as the longest mine has lasted is a week – and that was when I started out with 8 cups. Yes, that was a lot of tomatoes.

FABULOUS QUESADILLAS
1 small onion, thinly sliced
spinach, washed and chopped
tortilla
pepper jack cheese, optional
fresh tomato

Saute the onion. Then add the spinach. When the spinach is wilted, serve it over the tortilla. Top with cheese, if using, two slices of fresh tomato per quesadilla, and serve!

REFRIED BEANS
cooked beans, mashed
fat
onion, optional
tomatoes, optional
chili, optional
salsa, optional

Put the cooked mashed beans (at least a cup) in a skillet with several tablespoons of fat. Heat and add salsa. Serve. If onion is desired, saute the onion before adding the beans.

TAMALES

For the longest time, I've been intimidated by the process of making tamales. Everyone agrees it's "hard" and is more of a cooking "project" than something you make when you want to eat. But reading various recipes for tamales, it didn't seem hard and I remember when my mother first got a food processor, she used it to make tamales on a fairly regular basis. So I made tamales. They weren't hard. They took a long time. The recipe I was using said to allow 3 hours for preparation. It took me all three hours. But then when you look at the recipe, it calls for 6! cups of masa harina!!! Anything that calls for 6 cups of flour is just asking for large volumes. I noticed that if I had halved the recipe, I would have been finished making the tamales long before I was tired, and we would have had enough for dinner rather than enough for dinner and enough to freeze and eat for dinner another time. The recipe I worked off of said that is produced 24 tamales. When I carefully measured 2 teaspoons of Masa and 2 teaspoons of filling, as the recipe instructed, it made 37 adorable tamales and I had lots of left over dried corn husks. Which, of course, have to be tossed as they don't keep if they aren't dried. The next time I make tamales, I will halve the recipe and I think I will wait until the summer when I have fresh corn husks available. I will also request my husband help me because he's great with detail oriented tasks that require patience. Filling corn husks with masa, filling, rolling and tying them is definitely on of those tasks.

CORN HUSKS

fresh corn husks, at least 36 large husks plus smaller strips for tying

or

1 6 ounce package dried corn husks

If using fresh corn husks, rinse them to remove dirt and corn silk. Pat them dry and then use as directed in the assembly of tamales. If using the dried corn husks, completely submerge them in warm water for at least 30 minutes to return them to a soft, pliable state. Rinse them to remove any residual dirt and corn silk, then cover them with hot water until ready to use them.

MASA

6 cups masa harina

1 tablespoon salt

1 2/3 cups oil

5 1/2 cups water, more if needed

Combine the masa harina and salt in a large stand mixer with the paddle attachment. Add the oil, followed by the water. I used only 5 cups of water. Add only enough water so that the dough resembles moist cookie dough.

FILLING

plain pinto beans, mashed

or

chopped kale and minced onion

or

sliced zucchini with sauteed leeks

Whatever filling you decide on, make sure it is well cooked and not juicy. It is helpful if you can measure it with a tablespoon so that you aren't overwhelming with tamale with an over bountiful filling.

ASSEMBLY

Clear a workspace with enough space for the large mixing bowl of masa, a large bowl for the wrapped tamales, the bowl of corn husks, the filling and a place to assemble everything. Take a large pliable corn husk and spread 2 ounces of masa in a roughly rectangular shape slightly less than ¼ inch thick. Place 2 tablespoons of filling in the center of the masa, then roll the corn husk so that the masa meets in the center, around the filling. Be sure to press the filling together on the ends so that it is completely encased and no filling is showing through the masa. Then wrap the tamale in the corn husk and either fold the ends so the corn husk is a cylinder shape with folded over ends, or use a thin strip of corn husk to tie each end so that the tamale resembles the shape of wrapped hard candy. When you have used up the masa and the filling, place the tamales in a steamer, leaving room between them for the each tamale to be evenly steamed, and steam them over simmering water for an hour and to an hour and a half. You will know the tamales are done when the masa no longer sticks to the corn husk. If you will not be eating the tamales within a day, freeze them until ready to use and place them directly from the freezer into the steamer. Serve the tamales warm with red chili sauce, the same used for making enchiladas, green chili sauce or salsa. Let each guest remove the corn husk from the tamale before covering it with sauce.

KALE TAMALE FILLING
kale, chopped
onion, minced
salt to taste
red chili flakes, also known as chili pequin, to taste

Wash and chop a bunch of kale. Saute a minced onion, then add the kale. When the kale is tender and has released all it's juices, add the salt and chili flakes.

ZUCCHINI TAMALE FILLING
leek, sliced
4 small zucchini, sliced
salt to taste
green chili powder to taste

Wash and thinly slice the leek and the zucchini. Saute the leek, then add the zucchini. When the zucchini is tender and has released all it's juices, add the salt and green chili.

CORINNA'S TORTILLA RECIPE
When I was quite little I remember sitting on the cabinet (the bowl was almost as tall as I was sitting there) watching my grandmother Corinna make these. When I was a little older I remember her having me memorize the recipe because **everyone** should know how to make tortillas without needed to look up a recipe!

3 cups flour
1 teaspoon salt
1 teaspoon baking powder
1 cup water
1 tablespoon oil

Mix the dry ingredients and heap them in a bowl. Form a well in the center. Pour the water and oil into the well and knead the dough, but not too much or they will be tough. Pull off balls of dough and roll them out. Cook on a flat cast iron griddle with no fat, hot enough that a drop of water jumps when it comes into contact with the griddle. Watch the tortilla puff up on the griddle, flip it when it's puffy and cook it on the other side.

9 DESSERTS YOU WON'T HAVE TO DESERT

BAKED APPLES
apples
apple juice
1 teaspoon cinnamon
Slice apples, enough to fill a 3 quart baking pan. Cover with apple juice and 1 teaspoon cinnamon. Bake until golden at 350 for an hour or 425 for 20-40 minutes.

APRICOT CANDY
This makes a lovely fruit leather or fruit roll up!
¼ cup – 3 cups dried apricots, depending on how much you want
Put dried apricots in a food processor until a paste is formed. Between two sheets of parchment paper, roll the paste to a thin translucent sheet. Dry out sheet by exposing first one side, then the other to open air approximately 8 hours at a time. Cut into strips and enjoy!

FROZEN TREATS, FROSTING, ICINGS OR SAUCES

FROZEN BANANAS
In the first grade, our teacher had us make a cookbook as a mother's day present for our parents. Incidentally, it also required us to practice our best handwriting. This recipe is the only one I recall and I particularly remember my pride in making it as my mother let me make it immediately upon bringing home the finished book.
bananas
walnuts, crushed
cinnamon (optional and mixed with the walnuts if using)
Peel bananas. Roll them in crushed walnuts. Freeze for at least an hour.

QUICK BANANA FLAVORED FROZEN TREATS
Blend a frozen. banana with frozen. peaches or strawberries, or cinnamon and walnuts to make various ice cream like substances.

BANANA PEACH FREEZE
Puree until smooth:
3 frozen bananas
8-12 frozen peach slices
Serve immediately.

STRAWBERRY GELATO
¾ cup frozen strawberries
¾ cup frozen raspberries
a drizzle of agave nectar
juice from 1 orange
enough water to form soft serve consistency
Combine everything, except the water in the food processor. Add a tablespoon of water at time. Serve immediately.

LEMON GRANITA
3 cups water
1 cup lemon juice
1/3 cup sugar, or to taste
Place all the ingredients in a metal dish in the freezer. Break up ice crystals with a fork every thirty minutes until the consistency of sherbert is achieved. Enjoy immediately or transfer to an airtight dish and keep for at most a week.

SUMMER ICES
Each set of ingredients, when combined in a blender makes a tasty frozen treat:
2 oz. frozen wild blueberries, 2 oz. frozen raspberries, 1 cup grape juice;
4-6 oz. frozen wild blueberries, 2-4 oz. frozen raspberries, 4-6 oz. frozen strawberries, 10-14 almonds, water to desired thickness, fructose to taste;

BANANA CINNAMON ICE CREAM
Blend, and then immediately serve:
3 frozen bananas
4 drops vanilla extract
¼ teaspoon cinnamon

BERRY SHERBERT
1 package. frozen strawberries,

1 package frozen blueberries

½ package frozen raspberries

plus a little apple or white grape juice in the food processor = yummy dessert!

Blending frozen berries with a little water or grape juice has also produced nice sherbert like substances.

DESSERT SALADS, SANDWICHES AND OTHER LAYERED DISHES

FRUIT COCKTAIL

This dish was invented when I was pregnant and very particular about what I would and would not eat.

fresh pineapple

½ bag frozen cherries (about 5 oz.)

several tablespoons of lemon juice.

Stir thoroughly so that every piece of pineapple and cherry is coated with lemon juice to off-set the sweetness and the lemon juice at the bottom is thoroughly mixed with juice from the pineapple and melting cherries so as to not be too sour.

CANNOLI SHELLS

Lois Dieterly (author of Sinfully Vegan) has a daughter who had the idea of making cannoli shells out of bananas. When I first read her recipe, I was worried these would turn brown or taste too much like banana. They didn't and they don't. Her recipe invites the reader to spread as thinly as possible. We did and that is apparently thinner than she spread them because our first attempt was quite brittle and we were unable to fold it over the forms except for a small piece in the middle which was slightly thicker than the rest. Her recipe calls for 4 bananas and 1 teaspoon lemon juice. She also leaves out the vanilla and water.

6 ripe bananas (with sugar spots)

¼ teaspoon cinnamon

1000 milligrams vitamin C

2 teaspoons water

¾ teaspoon vanilla.

Put everything in the blender and push down until smooth. Spread on parchment paper about 1/8" thick. Place in dehydrator or oven on lowest setting with door propped open and leave it about 10 hours or over night. Cut into 1 " strips. Remove the parchment paper. Wrap around cannoli forms or cream horn forms and cool. As this cools it will become a brittle shell.

PEAR CREAM

I saw a recipe for a pear walnut "bisque" once. Of course, I had to look up bisque on wikipedia and discovered that it refers to a seafood dish, which, of course, has never had any appeal for me. It made me wonder about a pear walnut soup and I discovered I had no walnuts, but I did have pine nuts, and cinnamon, and vanilla. I wrote down what I did as I went a long and instead of a yucky bisque we had a lovely cinnamon pear dish the consistency of soft peaked whipped cream – perfect for Elena to snack on or to use in cannolis!

1 ripe pear
1 scant cup pine nuts
½ teaspoon cinnamon
½ teaspoon vanilla

Combine everything in the food processor with the "s" blade attachment. The pear will oxidize and turn brown which works well with the strong taste of cinnamon, but if you prefer something prettier, make the raspberry variation below or toss in a handful of cranberries or cranberry concentrate and add sweetener to taste.

RASPERRY PEAR CREAM

1 ripe pear
1 scant cup pine nuts
½ teaspoon vanilla
1 cup frozen raspberries

Combine everything in the food processor with the "s" blade attachment. This makes a beautiful pink cream that is a lovely topping for fruit salad!

STRAWBERRY FOOLE

strawberry sorbet (frozen strawberries in food processor with white grape juice served immediately)
cashew cheese
fresh berries, grapes and cherries!

Make strawberry sorbet and serve in clear glass dishes, topped with cashew cream and fresh fruit.

RAW TART

Crust:

1 ¼ cup raw organic macadamia nuts, frozen

1/8 teaspoon sea salt

½ teaspoon vanilla extract

Combine in the food processor until a ball of pastry dough form. If the macadamia nuts are not frozen, you will get macadamia nut butter, but if they are solidly frozen, then you will get a ball of dough. Press dough into a tart pan using a tart tamper or the back of a spoon.

Filling

fresh raspberries.

I found when the raspberries are Silferleaf farm's Caroline variety and ripe enough that they come off the cane when your hand brushes them but not so ripe that ants or other little buggies have started munching on them, the raspberries themselves taste like jam and no additional sweetener is necessary.

This might be better in individual tart pans for a party as the first piece (like the first piece of many things) is difficult to extract. Also a scoop of vanilla bean ice cream or a layer of carob glaze between crust and raspberries transforms it from "quite good!" to "divine!!!!!" mmmm.... fresh raspberry tart... :-)

ALMOND
  CANNOLI CREAM, 162

  ORIGINAL VALENTINE
  DREAM CAKE, 162

  STRAWBERRY ALMOND
  SOUP, 20

ALMOND:, 20
APPLE
  APPLE FACES, 43

  XE "GLUTEN FREE:APPLE PIE
  FILLING"APPLE PIE FILLING,
  160

  XE "CINNAMON:SPICED
  APPLESAUCE"SPICED
  APPLESAUCE, 18

  XE "ALMOND:STRAWBERRY
  ALMOND
  SOUP"STRAWBERRY
  ALMOND SOUP, 20

APPLE:, 20
APRICOT
  APRICOT CANDY, 160

ARUGULA
  XE "TOFU:ANDREW'S
  LASAGNA"ANDREW'S
  LASAGNA, 91

  BEST PESTO, 143

  XE "GARBANZO

BEAN:GARBANZO BEANS
WITH ARUGULA"GARBANZO
BEANS WITH ARUGULA, 89

GARBANZO BEANS WITH
ARUGULA, 52

PESTO, 35, 143

XE "BASIL:PESTO
DRESSING"PESTO DRESSING,
22

ASPARAGUS
  XE
  "VEGETABLE:ASPARAGUS"AS
  PARAGUS, 43

  ASPARAGUS SOUP, 44, 112

ASPARAGUS:, 32
AVOCADO
  KALE SALAD, 30

BANANA
  BANANA CINNAMON ICE
  CREAM, 161

  BANANA PEACH FRUIT
  FREEZE, 161

  XE "BLACKBERRY:BANANA
  SPLIT"BANANA SPLIT, 161

  FROZEN BANANAS, 160

BANANA:, 20
BASIL

XE "ARUGULA:BEST PESTO"BEST PESTO, 143

DELIGHTFUL TOMATO BASIL SOUP, 125

DINNER SALAD, 26

XE "CUCUMBER:GREEN GODDESS SALAD"GREEN GODDESS SALAD, 28

XE "ARUGULA:PESTO"PESTO, 35, 143

PESTO DRESSING, 22

BEAN
ALPHABET SOUP, 111

AUNT AURORA'S BEANS, 131, 150

BEAN BURRITO, 152

XE "CORN:BLACK BEAN SALAD"BLACK BEAN SALAD, 25

CHICOS AND BEANS, 131, 151

COSTA RICA STYLE BLACK BEANS, 132, 151

EL PATIO BURRITO, 86

GALLO PINTO, 88, 155

MAMA'S BEANS, 152

MINESTRONE SOUP, 116

POLENTA CASEROLE, 96

REFRIED BEANS, 157

XE "CORN:TAMALE PIE"TAMALE PIE, 103, 159

BEETS
XE "FENNEL:NORTHERN CALIFORNIA SPRING SALAD"NORTHERN CALIFORNIA SPRING SALAD, 32

PINK MASHED POTATOES, 58

BLACKBERRY
BANANA SPLIT, 161

XE "STRAWBERRY:FAVORITE FRUIT SALAD"FAVORITE FRUIT SALAD, 27

BLACKBERRY:, 20
BLUEBERRY
BLUEBERRY FOOLE, 163

BLUEBERRY:, 20, 27
BREAD
4 SEED CRACKER RECIPE, 79

BISCUITS LIKE MOM USED TO MAKE, 77

BREAD STICK VARIATION, 78

BREAD STICKS, 78

CORINNA'S TORTILLA RECIPE, 159

CRACKER VARIATION, 79

FRESH PASTA, 144

GREEN CHILE CRACKERS, 81

PITA, 81

PLOYES, 18

ROSEMARY BREAD STICKS, 78

SAGE BREAD, 64

SAVORY CRACKERS, 81

SUPER, 80

THYME BISCUITS, 19, 77

TORTILLAS, 82

BREAD:, 80
CAROB
XE "ALMOND:ORIGINAL VALENTINE DREAM CAKE "ORIGINAL VALENTINE DREAM CAKE, 162

CARROT
XE "COCONUT:CREAM OF CARROT SOUP"CREAM OF CARROT SOUP, 114

FALL CARROT SOUP, 115

MOROCCAN CARROT SALAD, 26

ROASTED CARROTS, 47

XE "POTATOES:ROASTED NEW POTATOES AND BABY CARROTS"ROASTED NEW POTATOES AND BABY CARROTS, 59

WINTER CARROT SOUP, 129

CASHEW
AVGOLEMONO SOUP, 112

XE "BLUEBERRY:BLUEBERRY FOOLE"BLUEBERRY FOOLE, 163

XE "CHEESE:CASHEW CHEESE"CASHEW CHEESE, 24

FAUX CREAM CHEESE, 24

RAW LASAGNA, 92

RAW PIZZA, 147

STRAWBERRY FOOLE, 163

CEREAL
ATOLE, 17

XE "CORN:CHAQUEWE"CHAQUEWE, 17

XE
"OAT:OATMEAL"OATMEAL,
18

CHEESE
BRAZIL NUT, 24

CASHEW CHEESE, 24

XE "CASHEW:FAUX CREAM
CHEESE"FAUX CREAM
CHEESE, 24

FRESH CHEESE, 24

XE "TOFU:TOFU "RICOTTA"
CHEESE"TOFU, 24

CHERRY
CHERRY PINEAPPLE
COCKTAIL, 162

CHERRY:, 20
CINNAMON
XE "PEARS:CINNAMON PEAR
CREAM"CINNAMON PEAR
CREAM, 163

SPICED APPLESAUCE, 18

COCONUT
CREAM OF CARROT SOUP,
114

XE "TOFU:PURPLE
SOUP"PURPLE SOUP, 123

THAI GINGER SOUP, 127

COCONUT:, 24, 27
CORN
XE "CEREAL:ATOLE"ATOLE,
17

BLACK BEAN SALAD, 25

CHAQUEWE, 17

ENCHILADAS, 87, 154

TAMALE PIE, 103, 159

TAMALES, 157

CUCUMBER
CUCUMBER HORS
d'OEUVRES, 49

CUCUMBER SALAD, 26

CUCUMBER SOUP, 115

GRAIN FREE SANDWICHES,
65

GREEN GODDESS SALAD, 28

JORDANIAN SALAD, 29

CURRY
GREEN CURRY (TOFU), 107

GREEN CURRY PASTE, 106

GREEN CURRY VARIATION,
107

GREEN CURRY VARIATION I,
107

INDIAN INSPIRED CURRY, 108

MUSAMUN CURRY (TOFU), 109

MUSAMUN CURRY PASTE, 109

RED CURRY PASTE, 109

THAI CURRY SAUCE, 106

YELLOW CURRY (TOFU), 111

YELLOW CURRY PASTE, 110

EGG
XE "TOFU:EGGLESS EGG SALAD"EGGLESS EGG SALAD, 87

EGGLESS EGG SALAD, 50

VEGAN FRITATTA, 51

EGGPLANT
BABA GANOUSH FOR A PARTY OF FORTY, 137

BHARTA, 85

KASHKE BADEMJAN, 140

SOLANACEAE PATTIES, 66, 103

EGGPLANT:, 91
FENNEL
XE "PEAS:FENNEL

PEAS"FENNEL PEAS, 55

FENNEL SALAD, 27

NORTHERN CALIFORNIA SPRING SALAD, 32

GARBANZO BEAN FALAFEL, 137

XE "ARUGULA:GARBANZO BEANS WITH ARUGULA"GARBANZO BEANS WITH ARUGULA, 52

GARBANZO BEANS WITH ARUGULA, 89

GREEN GARLIC HUMMUS, 139

HUMMUS, 139

PARSLEY HUMMUS, 140

GINGER
FAVORITE SUMMER SOUP, 125

XE "COCONUT:THAI GINGER SOUP"THAI GINGER SOUP, 127

GINGER:, 18
GLUTEN FREE
APPLE PIE FILLING, 160

EGGPLANT MANICOTTI, 91

XE "GARBANZO

169

BEAN:FALAFEL"FALAFEL, 137

XE "CUCUMBER:GRAIN FREE SANDWICHES"GRAIN FREE SANDWICHES, 65

MAI FUN NOODLES, 144

MILLET SALAD, 31

MILLET SALAD VARIATION, 31

PAD THAI INSPIRED ZUCCHINI PASTA, 95

PASTA PRIMAVERA, 145

RASPBERRY CAKE, 160

XE "CASHEW:RAW LASAGNA"RAW LASAGNA, 92

XE "CASHEW:RAW PIZZA"RAW PIZZA, 147

THAI ORCHID INSPIRED, 95

XE "PASTA:TUMERIA'S PASTA SALAD"TUMERIA'S PASTA SALAD, 33

GLUTEN FREE:, 163
GRAPE
  FRUIT SOUP, 20

GRAPE:, 20
LEMON
  BASIC VINEGRETTE, 22

LEMON GRANITA, 161

XE "VEGETABLE:SPRING VEGETABLES IN LEMON OLIVE OIL SAUCE"SPRING VEGETABLES IN LEMON OLIVE OIL SAUCE, 72

XE "SESAME SEED:TAHINI DRESSING"TAHINI DRESSING, 23

LEMON:, 162
MACADAMIA NUT
  XE "CHEESE:FRESH CHEESE"FRESH CHEESE, 24

XE "RASPBERRY:RASPBERRY TART WITH SHORTBREAD CRUST"RASPBERRY TART WITH SHORTBREAD CRUST, 163

SPINACH TARTINES, 68

SUMMER SALAD, 34

MISO SOUP, 117
MUSHROOMS
  MUSHROOM BURGERS, 53, 90

MUSHROOM GRAVY, 53

OYSTER MUSHROOMS IN THE HALF SHELL, 53

OAT
  OATMEAL, 18

OLIVE

    ANDREW'S SALAD, 25

    XE "LEMON:BASIC
    VINEGRETTE"BASIC
    VINEGRETTE, 22

    GREEK SALAD, 27

    GREEN OLIVE AND FRENCH
    LENTIL TAPENADE, 67

    MESCLUN SALAD, 31

    TABOULI SALAD FOR A
    PARTY OF FORTY, 141

OLIVE:, 23
ORANGE:, 20
PASTA
    TUMERIA'S PASTA SALAD, 33

PEACH
    XE "BANANA:BANANA
    PEACH FRUIT
    FREEZE"BANANA PEACH
    FRUIT FREEZE, 161

PEACH:, 20
PEARS
    CINNAMON PEAR CREAM,
    163

    XE "GRAPE:FRUIT
    SOUP"FRUIT SOUP, 20

    XE "RASPBERRY:RASPBERRY
    PEAR CREAM"RASPBERRY
    PEAR CREAM, 163

PEAS
    FENNEL PEAS, 55

    XE "POTATOES:INDIAN
    POTATOES"INDIAN
    POTATOES, 56

    INDIAN POTATOES, 98

    INDIAN POTATOES
    VARIATION, 57

    POTATOES AND PEAS!, 59

    ROSEMARY PEAS, 55

    SPLIT PEA SOUP, 135

PINEAPPLE
    XE "CHERRY:CHERRY
    PINEAPPLE
    COCKTAIL"CHERRY
    PINEAPPLE COCKTAIL, 162

PINEAPPLE:, 20
PIZZA
    ANDREW'S FAVORITE, 149

    XE "VEGETABLE:FAVORITE
    PIZZA TOPPING
    COMBINATIONS"FAVORITE
    PIZZA TOPPING
    COMBINATIONS, 148

    XE "VEGETABLE:WHO NEEDS
    CHEESE? VEGETABLE
    PIZZA"WHO NEEDS CHEESE?
    VEGETABLE PIZZA, 149

PIZZA:, 147
POLENTA, 96
POTATOES
    ALOO PARATHA, 76

    ALOO TIKKI, 43

    BASIC WINTER SOUP, 128

    BREAKFAST BURRITO, 86,
    153

    CORINNA'S POTATO SOUP,
    120

    GALETTE de POMMES de
    TERRE, 51

    GREEN BORSCHT, 113

    GREEN LENTIL STEW, 135

    GREEN MASHED POTATOES,
    57

    HEARTY POTATO SOUP, 121

    XE "PEAS:INDIAN
    POTATOES"INDIAN
    POTATOES, 98

    INDIAN POTATOES, 56

    XE "PEAS:INDIAN POTATOES
    VARIATION"INDIAN
    POTATOES VARIATION, 57

    LEMON BASIL MASHED
    POTATOES, 56

MASHED POTATOES, 57

MOTHER'S POTATO SOUP,
121

ORANGE MASHED
POTATOES, 57

PARSLEY POTATOES, 56

XE "BEETS:PINK MASHED
POTATOES"PINK MASHED
POTATOES, 58

POTATO SALAD, 60

POTATO SOUP, 122

XE "PEAS:POTATOES AND
PEAS!"POTATOES AND PEAS!,
59

ROASTED NEW POTATOES
AND BABY CARROTS, 59

ROASTED SPRING POTATOES
WITH ROSEMARY AND
GARLIC, 59

SAVORY KUGELESQUE DISH,
133

XE "EGGPLANT:SOLANACEAE
PATTIES"SOLANACEAE
PATTIES, 66, 103

WINTER ROOT VEGETABLE
SOUP, 129

XE "POTATOES:YELLOW MASHED POTATOES"YELLOW MASHED POTATOES, 58

YELLOW MASHED POTATOES, 58

PUMPKIN
PUMPKIN ACORN SQUASH SOUP, 123

PUMPKIN SOUP, 123

PUMPKIN SOUP VARIATION, 123

QUINOA, 99
RASPBERRY
GLUTEN FREE XE "GLUTEN FREE:RASPBERRY CAKE"RASPBERRY CAKE, 160

RASPBERRY PEAR CREAM, 163

RASPBERRY TART WITH SHORTBREAD CRUST, 163

RASPBERRY:, 20, 27
RICE
ARROZ CON PALMITO, 85, 150

XE "BEAN:GALLO PINTO"GALLO PINTO, 88, 155

POTLUCK PERFECT RICE, 62, 101

RICE AND GREENS, 63, 101

SPANISH RICE, 64, 102

SANDWICHES, 65
SESAME SEED
SESAME NOODLES, 98

TAHINI DRESSING, 23

ZA'ATAR, 42, 142

SESAME SEED:, 23, 28, 32
SOUP
DAHL MIDDLE EASTERN STYLE, 115

STRAWBERRY
FAVORITE FRUIT SALAD, 27

XE "CASHEW:STRAWBERRY FOOLE"STRAWBERRY FOOLE, 163

STRAWBERRY GELATO, 161

STRAWBERRY:, 20
SUNFLOWER SEEDS
RAW XE "GLUTEN FREE:PASTA PRIMAVERA"PASTA PRIMAVERA, 145

SUN-DRIED TOMATO SUNFLOWER SEED PATE, 98

TOMATO, 41, 146

SUNFLOWER SEEDS:, 22, 143
TOFU

ANDREW'S LASAGNA, 91

DINNER BURRITO, 153

XE "EGG:EGGLESS EGG SALAD"EGGLESS EGG SALAD, 50

EGGLESS EGG SALAD, 87

XE "GLUTEN FREE:EGGPLANT MANICOTTI"EGGPLANT MANICOTTI, 91

XE "VEGETABLE:GREEN GARLIC STIR FRY"GREEN GARLIC STIR FRY, 37

MARINATED TOFU SALAD, 30

MISO SOUP VARIATION, 117

PAD THAI, 97

PURPLE SOUP, 123

SIMPLE YUMMY TOFU SCRAMBLE, 71, 105

TOFU, 24

TOFU SCRAMBLE, 70

TOFU SCRAMBLE - GREEK STYLE, 70, 104

TOMATO
    RANCHOS SALSA, 41

VEGETABLE
    ALOO SAAG, 84

ASPARAGUS, 43

BRIGHT SQUASH, 66

BROCCOLI, 46

CANDIED YAMS, 73

CELERY ROOT PUREE, 49

CELERY STICK RACE CARS, 47

CHILI ONIONS, 54

DUSHENKA'S NOT- HOT SALSA, 40, 155

FAVORITE PIZZA TOPPING COMBINATIONS, 148

GREEN BEANS, 52, 89

GREEN CHILI, 36

GREEN GARLIC, 36

GREEN GARLIC STIR FRY, 37

XE "OLIVE:GREEN OLIVE AND FRENCH LENTIL TAPENADE"GREEN OLIVE AND FRENCH LENTIL TAPENADE, 67

KELITE, 52

PASTA WITH VEGETABLES,

93, 145

PEAS, 55

QUINOA WITH VEGETABLES, 61, 100

ROASTED BRUSSEL SPROUTS, 46

XE "CARROT:ROASTED CARROTS"ROASTED CARROTS, 47

ROASTED PARSNIPS, 54

ROASTED RED PEPPERS, 55

ROASTED VEGETABLE TORTE, 71

SALAD SOUP, 124

SAVORY SQUASH TART, 104

SPINACH WITH ONIONS, 66

SPRING VEGETABLES IN LEMON OLIVE OIL SAUCE, 72

STEAMED YAMS, 74

STUFFED ROMA TOMATOES, 69

SUGAR SNAP PEAS, 103

TENDER SUMMERY GOODNESS, 71

VERDOLAGAS, 73

WHO NEEDS CHEESE? VEGETABLE PIZZA, 149

VEGETABLE:, 92
ZUCCHINI CALABACITAS, 48

LUNCH BURRITO, 153

XE "GLUTEN FREE:PAD THAI INSPIRED ZUCCHINI PASTA"PAD THAI INSPIRED ZUCCHINI PASTA, 95

ZUCCHINI TAMALE FILLING, 159

ZUCCHINI:, 145

ABOUT THE AUTHOR

Dushenka Silberfarb grew up in New Mexico and went to college in Southern California. After graduating with a degree in theoretical mathematics, she returned to Albuquerque, where she met her husband. They lived in Pasadena and then Menlo Park before moving to the Boston area where their first child was born. Her cuisine is heavily influenced by the local foods available in the places she has lived or visited, her vegan mother, and the foods she ate while dating her husband. She also reads cookbooks for fun and enjoys creating organic plant based healthy delicious versions of recipes that call for dairy, meat or sugar in their original forms.